THE STORY OF THE
PERSIAN WAR

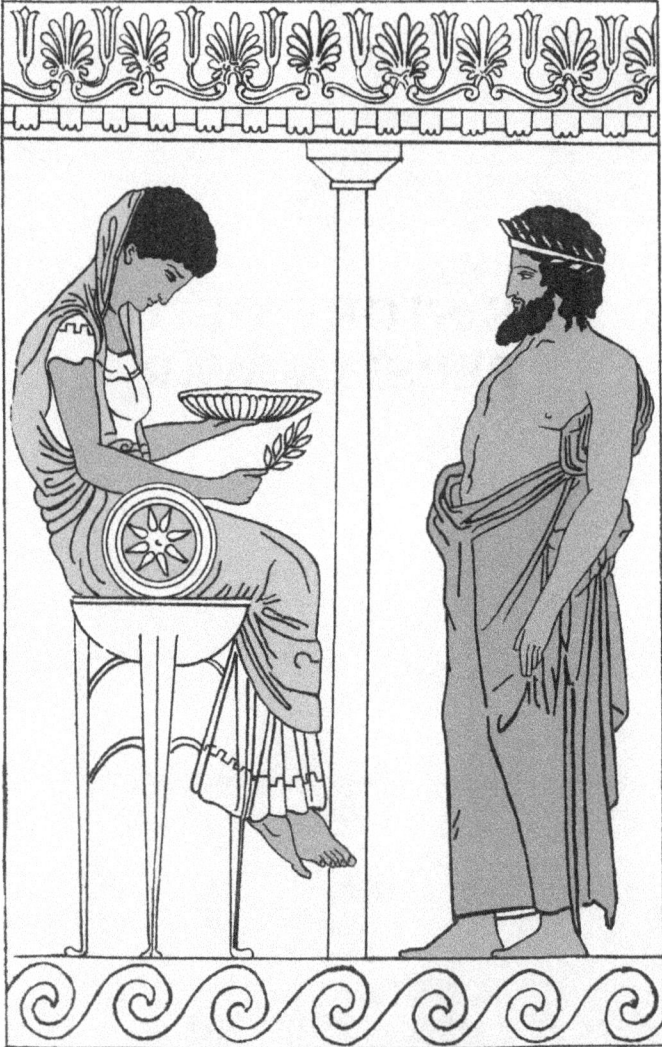

THE ORACLE

THE STORY OF THE PERSIAN WAR

FROM HERODOTUS

BY

Alfred J. Church

YESTERDAY'S CLASSICS

CHAPEL HILL, NORTH CAROLINA

This edition, first published in 2009 by Yesterday's Classics, an imprint of Yesterday's Classics, LLC, is an unabridged republication of the text originally published by Dodd, Mead and Company in 1881. For the complete listing of the books that are published by Yesterday's Classics, please visit www.yesterdaysclassics.com. Yesterday's Classics is the publishing arm of the Baldwin Online Children's Literature Project which presents the complete text of hundreds of classic books for children at www.mainlesson.com.

ISBN-10: 1-59915-330-0

ISBN-13: 978-1-59915-330-8

Yesterday's Classics, LLC
PO Box 3418
Chapel Hill, NC 27515

CONTENTS

PREFACE

I FOUND that "The Story of the Persian War," if it was to be fully told, would require all the space at my command. I have not, therefore, gone beyond this subject, and have given to this book the title which best describes its contents. There are yet "Stories of the West" to be found in Herodotus, which I may have, I hope, an opportunity of giving to the public.

The illustrations of this volume are taken from various sculptures and vases. The artist has sought to reproduce in them the coloring of a certain small class of Greek pottery, examples of which may be seen in the British Museum.

ALFRED CHURCH.

HADLEY GREEN,
    Oct. 21, 1881.

TO
ALEXANDER MACMILLAN,
This Book
IS DEDICATED.

CHAPTER I

OF THE REVOLT OF MILETUS

KING DARIUS gave Myrcinus that is on the river Strymon, in the land of Thrace, to Histiæus, lord of Miletus, for a reward; for Histiæus had done him good service in his warfare against the Scythians. But when the man began to build a wall about the place, one said to the King, "O King, what is this that thou hast done, giving this city in Thrace to a man that is a Greek, and wise moreover and crafty? For in that country is great store of timber for ship-building, and mines also of silver and there are many inhabitants, both Greeks and barbarians, who will take this fellow for a leader, and will do what he shall bid them, working day and night. Do thou therefore stay him in this work; but stay him with soft words. Bid him come to thee, and when he is come, take good care that he never go among the Greeks any more." This counsel seemed good to the King. Wherefore he sent a messenger to Histiæus, saying, "Thus saith the King, I am persuaded that there is no better man disposed to me and to my kingdom than thou. Come therefore to me, for I have great matters in hand and would fain ask thy counsel about them." So Histiæus, taking these words to be true, and counting it a great thing to be the

King's counselor, came to Sardis to Darius. And when he was come, Darius said to him, "Hear now the cause wherefore I have sent for thee. Since the day that thou didst depart from me I have desired nothing so much as to see thee and talk with thee; for in my judgment there is nothing so precious as a friend that is both faithful and wise; and this I know thee to be. Leave now thy city of Miletus, and that also which thou art building in Thrace, and come with me to Susa, for all that I have is thine, and thou shalt live with me, and be my counselor."

After this the King went up to Susa, taking Histiæus with him. And he left Otanes to be captain of them that dwell by the sea. This Otanes was the son of a certain Sisamnes whom, being one of the royal judges, and having given unrighteous judgment for money, King Cambyses slew; and having slain him, he flayed off his skin, and cutting it into strips stretched them on the judgment-seat. And making the son of Sisamnes to be judge in his father's room, he bade him remember on what manner of seat he sat.

In these days Miletus was the most prosperous of all the cities of Ionia, though it had been brought very low in the second generation before by strife among its citizens. This strife was healed after this fashion by the Parians, whom the men of Miletus chose out of all the Greeks to be judges in their case. These Parians went through the land of Miletus, and wheresoever they saw in the country, which was for the most part desolate, any field well tilled, they wrote down the name of the master of the field. And when they had traversed the whole, and found not many such, so soon as they were come back to the city, they called an assembly, and made this award, that the men whose fields they had seen to be well tilled should bear rule, for they judged that such as managed well their own affairs would manage well the affairs of the State also. But now from this city of Miletus, and from the island of Naxos, which was the richest of all the islands, there came great damage to the men of Ionia. It happened on this wise. Certain of the rich men of Naxos, being banished by the commons, fled to Miletus, of which city one Aristagoras was lord in those days, being son-in-law to Histiæus. And when the exiles prayed him for help that they might come back to their own country, Aristagoras, thinking that if they should come back by his help, he should be lord of Naxos, said to them (and he had this pretext for helping them that they had been long time friends of his father-in-law), "I cannot bring you back to Naxos against the will of the city, for I hear that they have eight thousand men at arms, and many ships of war. But I have a friendship with Otanes, that is brother to King Darius, and captain of them that dwell by the sea, and has many soldiers and ships. I will work with him that he shall do what ye wish." To this the exiles agreed, saying that they would find pay for the army. Then went Aristagoras to Otanes and said to him, "There is a certain island of Naxos, not very great, but a good land and fair, and near to Ionia, and having in it much wealth and many slaves. If thou wilt make war upon this island, bringing back to it certain men that have been banished, thou shalt receive much wealth from me, over and above the cost of the war, for this it is just that we who desire it should pay; also thou wilt win for the King Naxos and the islands that are subject to it, and from thence thou wilt be able to make war on Eubœa, a great island and a rich, being not less than Cyprus, and easy to be subdued. For all this a hundred ships will be sufficient." To this Otanes made answer, "Truly thou bringest a matter that may advantage the house of the King, and thy counsel is good, save as to the number of the ships. There shall be ready not one hundred but two hundred in the spring season. Only the King must approve of the undertaking." And when he had sent to the King and had his assent, he made ready two hundred ships of war, putting on them a great multitude of Persians and allies, and setting Megabates, that was nephew to him and to the King, to command them. (It was the daughter of this Megabates that Pausanias the Spartan would have taken to wife, if indeed the story be true, when he sought to make himself lord of Greece.) Megabates took with him Aristagoras, and many soldiers from Miletus, and the exiles, and sailed towards the Hellespont. But when he came to Chios he cast anchor, waiting for a north wind that he might sail to Naxos. And here—for it was not to be that Naxos should perish at this time—there befell this thing.

As Megabates went about visiting the watches of the fleet, he found a ship of Myndus in Caria, that had no watch set. Being very wroth at this, he bade his guards find the captain of the ship (the man's name was Scylax), and bind him in one of the tholes of the oars, so that his head should be without the ship and his body within. When the man had been so bound, there came one to Aristagoras saying that Megabates had bound Scylax of Myndus in a shameful fashion. Then Aristagoras entreated of Megabates that he would loose him; but, as he could not prevail, he loosed the man himself. When Megabates heard it he was very wroth with Aristagoras, who said to him, "What hast thou to do with these things? Wast thou not sent to do my pleasure, and to sail whithersoever I should bid thee? Meddle not then with other men's matters." Then Megabates, in his anger, sent a messenger to the Naxians, so soon as it was night, telling them what was preparing against them. Now these had not thought of any such thing; but when they heard it, forthwith they carried their goods from out of the fields into the city, and prepared themselves for a siege, making provision of food and drink. When therefore the Persians were come from Chios, they found the city of the Naxians defended against them; and having besieged it to no purpose for four months, when now all the money they had brought with them was spent, and much also that Aristagoras had furnished, they departed, having first built forts for the exiles. Then Aristagoras was in a great strait, for he could not fulfill the promise that he had made to the servants of the King, neither could he pay the money that had been spent upon the war, and he feared lest, falling into ill-favor with the Persians, being already at enmity with Megabates, he should lose the lordship of Miletus. For these causes he had it in his mind to revolt from the King. And while he thought thereon there came to him the man with the branded head from Histiæus at Susa, with a message that he should do this very thing. For Histiæus, seeking to send word to Aristagoras, yet not being able to send it safely, because the roads were guarded, devised this thing. He took the most faithful of his slaves and, shaving the man's head, branded on it certain letters. And when the hair was grown again he sent him to Aristagoras with a message, "Look on this man's head when thou hast shaven it." Now the marks signified that he should revolt. And this Histiæus did, counting it a grievous thing that he was constrained to tarry at Susa; for he said to himself, "If there be rebellion at Miletus, doubtless I shall be sent down to the sea; but if not, I shall go there no more." Then Aristagoras took counsel with his fellows, declaring to them his own judgment and the message that had come to him from Susa. To them spake Hecatæus, the writer of chronicles. First he counseled them not to make war against the King, telling them of all the nations that he ruled and of his might. And when he could not persuade them, he said that they should certainly make themselves masters of the sea, and that this they could do only by laying hands on the treasures that had been given by Crœsus the Lydian to the temple of Apollo at Branchidæ, for these were very great, "since I have good hope," said he, "that by help of these ye may have the upper hand at sea; any how, ye will have the using of them, and they will not be a spoil to the enemy." But neither in this could he prevail. Nevertheless they made ready to revolt. And first of all they sent and laid hands by guile on the captains of the ships that had sailed against Naxos. Such of these men as were lords of their cities Aristagoras gave into the hands of their citizens to do with them as they would. And he gave up his own lordship at Miletus. Thus lordship ceased out of all the cities of Ionia.

After this Aristagoras sailed to Sparta, for he had need to make alliance with some city that could help him. Now Cleomenes was King at Sparta in those days; to him therefore Aristagoras opened the matter, saying, "Marvel not, Cleomenes, that I have been at the pain to come hither. That we men of Ionia should be slaves and not free is a shame and grief, first indeed to us, but next to you more than all others, seeing that ye have the pre-eminence in Greece. Do ye therefore deliver us from slavery, seeing that we are of the same blood with you. And this ye can easily do, for these barbarians have but small courage, in which ye, I know, excel. Their manner of fighting is this. They have bows and short spears, and for clothing they have loose tunics and turbans on their heads. Think then how easily ye can subdue them." After this Aristagoras showed to the King the divers nations and countries that were obedient to the Persians, for he had a tablet of brass on which was engraven the whole compass of the world, with the sea and all the rivers. And he set forth to him in what things each was excellent, till he came at the last to the city of Susa. "Here," he said, "is the river Choaspes with the great city of Susa, where the King has his palace. Here also are his treasures, on which if ye can lay your hands ye may without fear compare yourselves for riches to Zeus himself. What profit is there to fight, and that many times, for a few furlongs of barren land, with Messenians, men that are your match, or with Arcadians or Argives that have not gold or silver or any such thing, for the getting of which a man might willingly go in peril of his life, and this when ye might be lords of all Asia?" Then said Cleomenes, "Man of Miletus, I will give thee an answer in this matter on the third day." And on the third, when they came together as had been appointed, the King said, "Tell me, Aristagoras, of how many days is the journey from the sea to this city of Susa?" Now in every thing else Aristagoras had answered him craftily; but in this he was taken unawares. For if he would have had the Spartans come to Asia, he should not have told the truth; but this he did tell, for he said, "It is a journey of three months." But when the King heard this he would not suffer Aristagoras to say what he would have told about the journey, but cried, "Man of Miletus, depart from Sparta before the setting of the sun; for thou hast nothing to say that can profit the Spartans if thou wouldst take them a journey of three months from the sea." When he had said this, the King departed to his house. Then Aristagoras, taking the garb of a suppliant, went to him and besought him, as he had regard to a suppliant, to listen to him. "But first," he said, "send away the child;" for there stood by the King his little daughter, whose name was Gorgo. This Gorgo was his only child, being now of eight or nine years. But Cleomenes bade him say what he would, and stay not for the child. Then Aristagoras began with ten talents, promising that he would give him so much if he would help him to that which he desired. And when Cleomenes would not, he promised yet more, till he came to fifty talents. Then the child spake, "Father, this stranger will corrupt thee unless thou rise up and depart." This counsel of the child greatly pleased Cleomenes, so that he rose up from his place and went into another chamber. After this Aristagoras departed from Sparta, and came to Athens, knowing that this city held the next place for power.

CHAPTER II

OF THE TAKING OF MILETUS

THE city of Athens had greatly increased in might since it was rid of its lords. The manner of the riddance was this. For a while after Hipparchus had been slain—this Hipparchus, with Hippias his brother, had received the lordship from Pisistratus his father, and he had been slain at the festival of Athene—the tyranny was more grievous than before. Now there was in Athens a great house, the sons of Alcmæon, and these had been banished by the children of Pisistratus. At the first indeed joining with others who were in like case, they sought to obtain their return by force, building a fort on Mount Parnes, whence they might attack the city; but they accomplished nothing. Then they devised this device. They made a covenant with the council of the Amphictyons that they would build the temple of Apollo that is in Delphi for a certain sum of money. But in the building they made all things fairer than according to the letter of the covenant—and this they could do by reason of their great wealth—and especially, when it had been agreed that they should use common stone in the building of the temple, they used for the front thereof marble of Paros. After this they persuaded the Pythia with a sum of money that whenever any men from Sparta came to ask counsel of the oracle, whether they came on their own affairs or the affairs of the State, she should bid them set free the city of Athens. When this message had come to the Lacedæmonians many times, they sent one of their chief citizens with an army to drive out the children of Pisistratus from Athens. And this they did, though the men were dear friends to them, for they judged it well to prefer the bidding of the Gods to the friendship of men. This army came by sea and landed at Phalerus. And when the sons of Pisistratus heard of it, they sent for help to Thessaly, with which country they had alliance, and there came to them from Thessaly a thousand horsemen, under Cineas, King of Thessaly. With them they assailed the camp of the Lacedæmonians, and slew not a few of them, among whom was the captain of the army, and drove such as were left into their ships. After this the Lacedæmonians sent another army, greater than before, under King Cleomenes, sending them not in ships but by land. These also, so soon as they had crossed the borders, the horsemen of the Thessalians attacked, but could not stand before them, but fled back without delay into their own land. Then Cleomenes, coming to the city and taking to him such as were minded to drive out from Athens its lords, besieged the sons of Pisistratus in the Pelasgian fort; but they would not have accomplished their purpose—for they had no mind to make a long siege of the fort, and the sons of Pisistratus had meat and drink in abundance—but would have tarried a few days, and so departed, but for this chance.

The sons of Pisistratus sought to send their children out of the country secretly; but the children were taken. Then they made a covenant with the Athenians that, if the children should be given back to them, they would depart out of the country within the space of five days. And this they did, their house having had the lordship for thirty years and six. Thus was Athens rid of its lords.

THE FESTIVAL OF ATHENE: HORSEMEN

Aristagoras then coming to this city of Athens presented himself before the people, and said the same words that he had said before in Sparta, about the good things in Asia, and about the manner of fighting of the Persians, how they had neither spear nor shield, and were therefore easily to be conquered. Also he said that the Milesians were colonists from Athens, and that it was just that the Athenians, being so mighty, should deliver them from slavery. And because his need was great, there was nothing that he did not promise, till at the last he persuaded them. For it is easier, it seems, to deceive a multitude than to deceive one man. Cleomenes the Spartan, being but one man, Aristagoras could not deceive; but he brought over to his purpose the people of Athens, being thirty thousand. So the Athenians, being persuaded, made a decree to send twenty ships to help the men of Ionia, and appointed one Melanthius, a man of reputation among them, to be captain. These ships were the beginning of trouble both to the Greeks and the barbarians.

THE FESTIVAL OF ATHENE: BRANCHBEARERS

After this Aristagoras sailed to Miletus; and so soon as he was gone there he did a thing which could be of no profit to the men of Ionia, but vexed King Darius. He sent a messenger to the Pæonians, whom Megabazus had carried away captive from the river Strymon and set down in Phrygia, saying, "Thus saith

Aristagoras, lord of Miletus, If ye will obey him, ye shall have deliverance. All Ionia hath rebelled against the King. Now therefore ye can depart in safety to your own land. How ye shall get to the sea ye must order for yourselves; but when ye are come thither, we will see to the matter." The Pæonians heard this with great gladness; and taking with them their wives and their children, they fled to the sea. Yet some of them were afraid and remained behind. And when they had come to the sea, they crossed over to Chios. And when they were already in Chios there came a multitude of the horsemen of the Persians, pursuing them, who, as they had not been able to overtake them, sent messengers to them in Chios, bidding them return to the land of Phrygia. But the Pæonians would not hearken to them. And the people of Chios carried them thence to Lesbos, and the Lesbians carried them to Doriscus; and from Doriscus they returned on foot to their own land of Pæonia.

When the twenty ships of the Athenians were arrived, and with them five ships of the Eretrians, which came, not for any love of the Athenians, but because the Milesians had helped them in old time against the men of Chalcis, Aristagoras sent an army against Sardis, but he himself abode in Miletus. This army, crossing Mount Tmolus, took the city of Sardis without any hindrance; but the citadel they took not, for Artaphernes held it with a great force of soldiers. But though they took the city they had not the plunder of it, and for this reason. The houses in Sardis were for the most part built of reeds, and such as were built of bricks had their roofs of reeds; and when a certain soldier set fire to one of these houses, the fire ran quickly from house to house till the whole city was consumed. And while the city was burning, such Lydians and Persians as were in it, seeing that they were cut off from escape (for the fire was in all the outskirts of the city), gathered together in haste to the market-place. Through this market-place flows the river Pactolus, which comes down from Mount Tmolus, having gold in its sands, and when it has passed out of the city it flows into the Hermus which flows into the sea. Here then the Lydians and Persians were gathered together, being constrained to defend themselves. And when the men of Ionia saw their enemies how many they were, and that these were preparing to give battle, they were stricken with fear, and fled out of the city to Mount Tmolus, and thence, when it was night, they went back to the sea. In this manner was burned the city of Sardis, and in it the great temple of the goddess Cybele, the burning of which temple was the cause, as said the Persians, for which afterward they burned the temples in Greece. Not long after came a host of Persians from beyond the river Halys; and when they found that the men of Ionia had departed from Sardis, they followed hard upon their track, and came up with them at Ephesus. And when the battle was joined, the men of Ionia fled before them. Many indeed were slain, and such as escaped were scattered, every man to his own city.

After this the ships of the Athenians departed and would not help the men of Ionia any more, though Aristagoras besought them to stay. Nevertheless the

Ionians ceased not from making preparations of war against the King, making to themselves allies, some by force and some by persuasion, as the cities of the Hellespont and many of the Carians and the island of Cyprus. For all Cyprus, save Amathus only, revolted from the King under Onesilus, brother of King Gorgus.

When King Darius heard that Sardis had been taken and burned with fire by the Ionians and the Athenians, with Aristagoras for leader, at the first he took no heed of the Ionians, as knowing that they would surely suffer for their deed, but he asked, "Who are these Athenians?" And when they told him he took a bow and shot an arrow into the air, saying, "O Zeus, grant that I may avenge myself on these Athenians." And he commanded his servant that every day, when his dinner was served, he should say three times, "Master, remember the Athenians." After this he called for Histiæus of Miletus, and said to him, "Histiæus, I hear that thy deputy to whom thou gavest over Miletus has rebelled, and has brought men from over the sea to help him, and, taking with him also certain of the Ionians (who verily shall suffer for their wrong-doing), has taken from me the city of Sardis. How can this have been done without thy counsel? Take heed lest the blame fall on thee." Then answered Histiæus, "What is this that thou hast said, that I should devise any evil against thee? For what do I lack being here with thee? If my deputy has done such things, he has done them of his own counsel. Yet do I scarce believe that he has done them. But if so, see what a thing thou hast done in taking me away from the coast country. Surely had I been yet there, no city had been

16

troubled. But now send me as speedily as may be to the land of the Ionians, that I may set all things in order as they were aforetime, and also deliver up this deputy, if he has so done, into thy hands. Verily, I swear by thy Gods, O King, that I will not put off the tunic which I shall wear on the day when I go down to the land of the Ionians, before I make the great island of Sardinia tributary to thee." So Darius let him go, commanding him when he had accomplished these things to come back to him at Susa.

Meanwhile the Persians took not a few cities of the Ionians and Æolians. But while they were busy about these, the Carians revolted from the King; whereupon the captains of the Persians led their army into Caria, and the men of Caria came out to meet them; and they met them at a certain place which is called the White Pillars, near to the river Mæander. Then there were many counsels among the Carians whereof the best was this, that they should cross the river and so contend with the Persians, having the river behind them, that so there being no escape for them if they fled, they might surpass themselves in courage. But this counsel did not prevail. Nevertheless, when the Persians had crossed the Mæander, the Carians fought against them, and the battle was exceedingly long and fierce. But at the last the Carians were vanquished, being overborne by numbers, so that there fell of them ten thousand. And when they that escaped—for many had fled to Labranda, where there is a great temple of Zeus and a grove of plane trees—were doubting whether they should yield themselves to the King or depart altogether from

Asia, there came to their help the men of Miletus with their allies. Thereupon the Carians, putting away their doubts altogether, fought with the Persians a second time, and were vanquished yet more grievously than before. But on this day the men of Miletus suffered the chief damage. And the Carians fought with the Persians yet again a third time; for, hearing that these were about to attack their cities one by one, they laid an ambush for them on the road to Pedasus. And the Persians, marching by night, fell into the ambush, and were utterly destroyed, they and their captains.

After these things, Aristagoras, seeing the power of the Persians, and having no more any hope to prevail over them—and indeed, for all that he had brought about so much trouble, he was of a poor spirit—called together his friends and said to them, "We must needs have some place of refuge, if we be driven out of Miletus. Shall we therefore go to Sardinia, or to Myrcinus on the river Strymon, which King Darius gave to Histiæus?"

To this Hecateus, the writer of chronicles, made answer, "Let Aristagoras build a fort in Leros (this Leros is an island thirty miles distant from Miletus) and dwell there quietly, if he be driven from Miletus. And hereafter he can come from Leros and set himself up again in Miletus."

But Aristagoras went to Myrcinus, and not long afterwards was slain while he besieged a certain city of the Thracians.

And now Histiæus came down from Susa to Sardis. When he was come to Sardis, Artaphernes the governor inquired of him the cause why the Ionians had rebelled, and when Histiæus said that he could not tell, Artaphernes said, for indeed he knew the whole matter, "The matter stands thus, Histiæus. Thou hast stitched the shoe and Aristagoras has put it on." When Histiæus heard this, and perceived that the thing was known, he fled to the coast. And first he went to Chios, where the people cast him into prison, but finding that he had rebelled against the King set him at liberty; and from Chios he went to Miletus; but the men of Miletus, being rid of one lord, even Aristagoras, were not minded to take to themselves another, and when he sought to make an entrance by night, they fought against him and wounded him in the thigh. After this, having got ships from the Lesbians, he laid wait at the Hellespont and seized all the ships that came forth from the Black Sea unless they would take service with him.

Now the Persians had gathered together a great host and a fleet also against Miletus; and the men of Miletus sent deputies to the Great Ionian Council. And the council resolved that they would not send an army to fight against the Persians, but that the cities should send all their ships, not leaving one behind, and that they should be assembled at Lade, which is an island near Miletus. So all the Ionians sent their ships, a hundred coming from Chios, and eighty from Miletus, and sixty from Lesbos. The number of the whole was three hundred and fifty and three. But the number of the ships of the barbarians was six hundred.

First the Persian captains sent for the lords of the Ionian cities whom Aristagoras had driven out, and said to them, "Now can ye do good service to the house of the King. Let each seek to draw away his own countrymen from the alliance of the Ionians; and let him tell them that they shall suffer no harm by reason of their revolt, but shall be in all points even as they were in former days. But if they be stubborn then shall they and their children be sold into slavery, and their land shall be given unto strangers." Then the lords sent messengers to tell these words to their countrymen; but these would not hearken or betray their allies. And each people thought that these promises were made to them only and not to the others.

Afterward divers councils were held by the captains of the fleet, in which, after others had set forth their opinions, Dionysius of Phocæa thus spake, "Ye men of Ionia, now are our fortunes on the razor's edge, whether we shall be free men or slaves, and slaves that are also runaways. If ye will endure for the time some hardness, ye will be able to prevail over your enemies and so be free forever; but if ye continue in your present slothfulness and disorder, there is no hope but that ye will suffer the wrath of the King when he shall avenge himself on you for your revolt. Be therefore persuaded by me and yield yourselves to my commands; for if ye fulfill these faithfully either will the Persians fly before us, or if they fight, will be utterly vanquished."

The Ionians hearkened to these words and committed themselves to Dionysius. And he every day made them move their ships in column, and practice with their oars, and exercise themselves in breaking the line. And the fighting men were kept under arms, and the ships remained on their anchors, so that the men had toil without ceasing from morning until night. These things the Ionians endured for seven days, but on the eighth—for they were not accustomed to such toil—being worn out with labor and with the heat of the sun, they began to say to each other, "Against what god have we sinned that we suffer such things? Surely we were mad that we gave ourselves to this boaster from Phocæa that has brought but three ships only. For he has taken us and plagued us with trouble that cannot be endured, so that many of us have already fallen sick, and many will soon fall. Surely it were better to endure any thing rather than these hardships. Even slavery were better than this servitude. Let us therefore yield him obedience no more."

After this they would not obey him, but pitched their tents upon the island, as though they had been soldiers, and lay in the shade, and would not practice themselves on their ships, which when the captains of the Samians perceived, they were more ready to receive the offer which the Persians had made to them. For they saw that there was no order among the Ionians, nor did they hope to prevail over the King, knowing that if they could vanquish this present fleet that was arrayed against them, there would come another five times as great. For this cause the Samians made an agreement with the King.

Not many days afterwards the ships of the Phœnicians sailed out to do battle, and the Ionians sailed against them. Who indeed bare themselves bravely and who played the coward that day is not certainly known, for the Ionians accused one another. But it is said that the Samians, according to the agreement that they had made, hoisted their sails and departed to Samos, but that eleven ships remained in their place and fought, for that the captains would not obey the leaders. For this deed the state of Samos granted them this honor, that their names should be written on a pillar, and that the pillar should be set up in the market-place of Samos. And this was done. Also the men of Lesbos, when they saw what their neighbors did, left also their place in the line; and indeed the greater part of the Ionians followed in the same way. Of them that remained the men of Chios were the most roughly handled. These had come with a hundred ships, on each of which were forty picked men at arms. Nor would they follow an ill example when they saw others play the coward, but behaved very valiantly, and though they were left well-nigh alone, yet broke many times through the lines of the enemy, and took many ships. And at the last, such as were able fled to Chios; and such as had their ships so sorely wounded that they could not return, beached their ships at this isle, and marched into the country of the Ephesians. This they did in the night, and the Ephesians, thinking that they were robbers that had come to steal away their women—for they were keeping a festival—marched out against them with their whole force and slew them.

As for Dionysius of Phocæa, when he saw that the Ionians were conquered, he would not return to Phocæa, for he knew that it must certainly fall into the hands of the Persians, but sailed away with his own ships and those that he had taken, and came to Phœnicia. There he sank certain merchantmen and took out of them a great booty. Afterwards he sailed to Sicily, and became a pirate, sparing indeed Greek ships, but taking ships of the Carthaginians and Tuscans.

WOMEN KEEPING FESTIVAL

The Persians besieged Miletus both by land and sea, digging mines under the walls, and using against it all manner of devices. And they took it in the sixth year from the time when Aristagoras caused it to revolt from the King. Most of the men they slew, and all the women and the children they made slaves; and the temple of Apollo at Branchidæ, to which, as has been said before, King Crœsus made many gifts, they burned with fire. Such of the inhabitants of Miletus as were not slain were sent up to Susa. The King did them no further harm, but settled them in the city of Ampe, which is near to the Red Sea, by the mouth of the river Tigris.

The Athenians showed what great sorrow they had

at the taking of Miletus by many other proofs, and especially by this. The poet Phrynichus made a play, "The Taking of Miletus;" but when he showed it on the stage the whole multitude in the theater wept. And they put a fine of a thousand drachmas upon him because he had called to mind, they said, their own misfortune. And they made a law that no one thereafter should show this play.

Not many days afterwards Histiæus was taken prisoner by the Persians. Doubtless, had he been sent to Susa, King Darius would have pardoned him. And indeed, for fear of this, Artaphernes, governor of Sardis, commanded him to be slain. His body he fastened on a stake, and his head he embalmed and sent it on to the King. When the King heard it, he greatly blamed the governor, because he had not sent him up alive; and he commanded that they should take the head, and dress it with all care, and so bury it, for that this man had been a great benefactor to the Persians.

After this the Persians took all the towns of the Greeks on the mainland of Asia, and they netted the islands. Now the manner of netting was this. The men joined hands, making a line across the island from north to south, and so passed through it from end to end, hunting out all the inhabitants. Thus were the cities of the Ionians enslaved for the third time, once by Crœsus, King of the Lydians, and twice by the Persians.

After this the King, having conquered the Ionians, bided his time till he should avenge himself upon the Athenians.

CHAPTER III

OF THE FIRST WAR AGAINST GREECE

Mardonius, the son of Gobryas, came down from Susa, and he had a great army and many ships. He was a young man, and he had newly married the daughter of King Darius. When he was come to the land of Cilicia, he took ship and sailed to the coast of Ionia, the other ships following him. And being in Ionia he did this thing (a marvelous thing, doubtless, in the eyes of them that believe not the story of Otanes, how he would have set up among the Persians the rule of the people); he cast down from their place all the lords of the Ionians, setting up in every city the rule of the people. When he had done this he went with all haste to the Hellespont, whither was gathered together a great multitude of ships and many thousands of men. These crossed the Hellespont in the ships, and so marched through the land of Europe. And their purpose was, as they said, to have vengeance on the cities of Athens and Eretria; but in truth they had it in their minds to subdue as many as they should be able of the cities of the Greeks. First, then, they subdued the Thrasians. These did not so much as lift a hand against the Persians, and so were

25

added to the nations whom they had in slavery. From Thasos they went to Acanthus, and leaving Acanthus they sought to pass round Mount Athos, which is a great promontory, running far out into the sea. Here there fell upon the ships a very mighty wind, such as they could in nowise bear up against, and did them much damage. Men say indeed that there perished of the ships three hundred, and of men more than twenty thousand. For the sea in these parts is full of great monsters, which laid hold on many of the men; many also were dashed against the rocks, and were so destroyed; and some perished because they could not swim, and some from cold. Thus it fared with the ships. As for Mardonius and his army, the Brygi, that are a tribe of Thracians, assailed him in his camp by night and slew many of his men, and wounded Mardonius himself. Notwithstanding, the Brygi escaped not the doom of slavery, for Mardonius left not this region till he had utterly subdued them. But when he had done this he went back to Asia, for his army had suffered much from the Thracians, and his ships from the storm at Mount Athos. Thus did this great undertaking come to an end with little honor.

For all this Darius changed not his purpose concerning Athens and the other cities of Greece. For every day, at his bidding, did his servant say to him, "O King, remember the Athenians." Also the children of Pisistratus ceased not to speak against the city. The King indeed desired, having for a pretense his quarrel against the Athenians, to subdue all the Greeks that would not give him earth and water; for the giving of these things is to the Persians a token of submission. Mardonius, seeing that he had fared badly in his undertaking, the King discharged of his office, appointing thereto Datis, that was a Mede, and Artaphernes his brother's son. These then he sent on the same errand on which he had sent Mardonius, saying to them, "Make slaves of the men of Eretria and of the men of Athens, and bring them to me that I may see them." So these two went down from the city of Susa to Cilicia, having with them a very great army and well-appointed; and while they were encamped here in a plain that is called the Aleian plain, there came also to that country the whole array of ships as had been commanded, and with the rest ships designed for the carriage of horses, for in the year before the King had commanded the inhabitants that such should be built. On these ships, therefore, they embarked their horses, and on the other ships the rest of the army, and so set sail to Ionia, having in all six hundred ships of war.

But they sailed not along the coast after the former manner, going northwards to the Hellespont and to Thrace, but voyaged through the islands, beginning with Samos; and this they did, as it seems, because they feared the going round Mount Athos, remembering what loss and damage they had suffered at this place in the former expedition. Also they had Naxos in their mind, for this had not as yet been conquered. They sailed, therefore, first to Naxos, and the people of the island did not abide their coming, but fled forthwith to the mountains. And the Persians made slaves of all on whom they could lay their hands, and burned the temples and the city with fire, and so departed. While they were doing these things the men of Delos left their island of Delos and fled to Tenos. But Datis suffered not the ships of the Persians to come to anchor at Delos, but bade them tarry over against it in Rhenea; and having heard where the men of Delos had bestowed themselves, he sent an herald, saying, "Holy men, why have ye fled from your dwelling-place, and have thought that which is not fitting concerning me? For indeed my own purpose and the commandment also which has been laid upon me by the King is this, that we should do no harm to the land in which the two Great Ones, Apollo and Artemis, were born, neither to it nor to the inhabitants thereof. Return ye therefore to your own dwellings and inhabit your island." This was the message which Datis sent to the men of Delos; and afterward he burned three hundred talents' weight of frankincense upon the altar of their temple. And it came to pass that when he had departed from Delos, the island was shaken by an earthquake. Now it had never been so shaken before, nor hath been since. This thing, without doubt, happened for a sign to the sons of men of the evils that were coming upon them. And indeed, in the days of Darius the son of Hystaspes, and Xerxes the son of Darius, and Artaxerxes the son of Xerxes, that were kings of Persia, the one after the other, there befell the Greeks worse evils than had befallen them for twenty generations before the days of Darius, of which evils some indeed came from the Persians and some from the chief among themselves when they contended together for the pre-eminence. Therefore it may well be believed that Delos had never been shaken before as it was shaken in these days.

From Delos the barbarians sailed to the other islands of that sea. And whithersoever they came they took some of the islanders to serve in the army and the ships, and of their children some to be hostages. But when they came to Carystus, the people of the land would not give hostages, neither were they willing to help in making war upon the cities of their neighbors, meaning thereby Eretria and Athens. Then the Persians besieged their town and laid waste their country till the men of Carystus agreed to do as had been required of them.

When the Eretrians heard that the Persians were coming against them with a great host and many ships, they sent to the Athenians praying for help. This the Athenians refused not to give, but sent to such of their citizens as had had land allotted to them in the country of the horse-breeding Chalcidians that they should go to the help of the men of Eretria. But these, though they sent this message to the Athenians, had no steadfast or worthy purpose in the matter. Some of them indeed were for leaving the city, that they might flee to the hill country of Euboea, but others, looking only to their own gain, and thinking that they should best get this from the Persians, made ready to betray their country. This, when Æschines the son of Nothus, than whom there was none greater in Eretria, heard, he told to the Athenians that had come the whole matter, and said to them: "Depart ye straightway to your own country, lest ye also perish." And the Athenians hearkened to the counsel of Æschines and departed, crossing the Oropus, and so got safe away. After this the ships of the Persians came to the land of Eretria, and put out the horses that they carried, and made ready as if they would fight with the enemy. But the Eretrians had no mind to come out of their walls and fight; only they hoped that they might perchance keep these against the enemy, for as to the counsel of leaving their city and fleeing to the hills, this they had given up. Then the Persians attacked the wall with great fury; and for six days they fought, many being slain on both sides; but on the seventh day, two men, of good repute among the citizens, whose names were Euphorbus and Philagrus, betrayed Eretria to the Persians; and these, entering into the city, first burned the temples, thereby revenging the burning of the temples of Sardis, and next made slaves of all the people, according as King Darius had given them commandment.

When they had thus dealt with Eretria, they sailed against Athens, having no doubt that they should speedily deal with this also after the same fashion. And seeing that Marathon was the most convenient for their purpose, and nearest also to Eretria, thither did Hippias the son of Pisistratus lead them. And the Athenians, so soon as they heard of their coming, marched with their whole force to Marathon. Ten generals they had, of whom the tenth was Miltiades the son of Cimon, the son of Stesagoras.

This Cimon had been banished from Athens by Pisistratus. And it chanced to him that as he went into banishment he won the prize at Olympia for the race of four-horse chariots. This same prize his half-brother Miltiades had also won. And in the next games at Olympia, being five years afterwards, he won again with the same mares; but granted to Pisistratus that his name should be proclaimed as the winner. Because he did this he came back to Athens under safe-conduct. And yet again he won the same prize with the same mares at the games next following; and having done this he was slain by the sons of Pisistratus, for Pisistratus himself was not yet alive. In the commonhall was he slain by men that were sent against him at night. He is buried before the City, beyond the road that is called the Hollow Road; and over against him are buried the mares that won for him these prizes. This same thing was done by other four mares, belonging to Evagoras the Lacedæmonian, but besides these none other have done it. This Cimon had two sons, of whom the elder, Stesagoras, was brought up by his friends in the Chersonese, and the younger, being named Miltiades, after this same uncle, was with his father in Athens.

THE CHARIOT RACE

This Miltiades then the Athenians had chosen with nine others to be general. But before this he had but narrowly escaped death. For first the Phœnicians pursued him so far as Imbros, being very desirous to lay hands upon him and to take him to the King. And when he had escaped from these, and, coming to his own country, believed that he was now in safety, his enemies brought him into judgment by reason of the lordship which he had had in the Chersonese. But these, too, he escaped, and the people chose him for their general.

CHAPTER IV

OF THE BATTLE OF MARATHON

FIRST of all the generals, before they led forth their army out of the city, sent a herald to Sparta, Pheidippides by name, who was an Athenian by birth, and by profession a runner, and one who had diligently exercised himself, and was very swift of foot. This man affirmed and declared to the Athenians that when he came in his running to Mount Parthenius, which is above Tegea, there met him the god Pan, and that Pan called him by his name, Pheidippides, and said to him: "Say to the Athenians, Why do they take no heed of me, though I am their friend, and have often done them good service in time past, and will do so hereafter." The Athenians, believing that this story was true, afterwards, when things had gone well with them, built a temple to the god Pan under the Acropolis, and honored him with yearly sacrifices and a procession of torches. Pheidippides then, being thus sent by the generals, came to Sparta on the next day, (Between Athens and Sparta there are one hundred and thirty and seven miles.) And so soon as he was come he went to the rulers and said: "O men of Sparta, the Athenians pray you that ye come and help them, and suffer not the most ancient city in the land of Greece to be brought into slavery by the barbarians. Already have they brought the men of Eretria into slavery, and Greece hath become the weaker by a famous city." This message did Pheidippides deliver to the Spartans. And to them when they heard it seemed good that they should help the men of Athens. Only they could not go to their help forthwith, because they would not break the law. For it was then but the ninth day of the moon; and on the ninth day it was unlawful for them, they said, to march, because the moon was not yet full. Therefore they waited for the full moon.

In the meantime Hippias the son of Pisistratus led the Persians to Marathon; and the prisoners from Eretria he landed on the island that is called Ægileia. And when the barbarians had disembarked from the ships, he busied himself with the setting of them in order. In the doing of this it happened to him to sneeze and cough with much violence; and, he being an old man, his teeth for the most part grievously shaken, and one of them he spat forth. This tooth fell into the sand, and he made much ado to find it, but could not. Seeing this he groaned, and said to them that stood by: "This land is not ours, neither shall we be able to subdue it; as for the share of it that was mine this tooth has taken it."

By this time the army of the Athenians was drawn up in the precinct of Hercules. To them being there there came the men of Platæa, every man that was able to bear arms. For the Platæans had before this time given themselves over to Athens, and the Athenians had by this time had no small trouble on their behalf.

The cause of the Platæans so giving themselves over was this. At the first, when they were pressed hard by the Thebans, they came to King Cleomenes, who chanced to be in their country, and would have given themselves over to him and the Lacedæmonians. But Cleomenes and his people would not receive them, saying: "We dwell in a country that is very far from you, and our help would be but of small avail to you. For indeed it might happen to you, and not once only, that ye should be made slaves, before any of us could so much as hear of the matter. Therefore we counsel you to give yourselves over to the men of Athens; seeing that they dwell close at hand and are good to help." This was the counsel of the Lacedæmonians, which they gave, not because they had any love for the men of Platæa, but thinking that the Athenians would have trouble without end if by these means they should be set at enmity with the Thebans. The men of Platæa willingly hearkened to their counsel, and sent envoys, who, journeying to Athens, sat themselves down on the altar and surrendered themselves, the Athenians keeping at this time the festival of the twelve gods. When the Thebans heard what had been done they marched against the men of Platæa; and on the other hand the Athenians came to their help. When these were now about to join battle, the Corinthians—for they chanced to be there—would not suffer them so to do, but made an agreement between them, both consenting thereunto. This agreement was that if any of the dwellers in Bœotia wished not to come into the league of Thebes, it should be lawful for them to stand aloof. When the Corinthians had given this sentence they departed to their own city. The Athenians also departed; but as they were on their way, the Thebans set upon them, but were worsted in the battle. Then the Athenians were no longer willing to abide by the boundaries which the Corinthians had determined for the men of Platæa, but took instead the river Asopus to be the boundary between them and the Thebans. So now the men of Platæa, being willing to make a return to the Athenians for the benefit which they had received, came to their help at Marathon.

FLUTE PLAYERS AND DANCERS

The generals of the Athenians were divided in their opinion, some being unwilling that they should join battle with the Persians, for they considered how few in numbers they were to stand against so great a host; but others, among whom was Miltiades, were for joining battle. Then, there being this division, as it seemed likely that the worse counsel would prevail, Miltiades went to the war-archon, whose name was Callimachus, a man of Aphidnæ. The war-archon among the Athenians was appointed by lot, and in former days it was the custom that he should vote together with the ten generals. To him therefore went Miltiades, and spake to him these words: "Thou hast it in thine hands, O Callimachus, either to bring Athens under the yoke of slavery, or to make it free for evermore, and in so doing to gain for thyself a name that shall never die, and glory such that not even Harmodius and Aristogeiton won for themselves. For indeed never since Athens was a city has it come into such danger as that wherein it now stands. For if it bow its neck to the yoke of the barbarian and be given over to this Hippias, what it will suffer thou knowest very well; but if it escape this danger, then will it become the very first city in the land of Greece. And now I will set forth to thee how these things may pass, and also how it lies with thee to determine whether they shall turn for the better or the worse. We generals are ten in number, and our opinions are divided, for some would have us join the battle with the Persians, and others would not. Now hear what will take place if we join not battle with these strangers forthwith. There will be a great dispute in the city, and the counsels of men will be turned aside from the right, so that the party of the Persians will prevail. But if we join battle before this evil begin to show itself, then I doubt not, if the Gods deal fairly with us, that we shall prevail in battle, and so be safe. And now all this lies upon thee, whether it shall be so or no. If thou wilt add thy vote to my vote, then shall this thy native country be free, and shall be the first city in all Greece. But if, on the other hand, they that be unwilling to fight shall gain the day, then shall happen to us the contrary of all the good things of which I have spoken." With these words Miltiades persuaded Callimachus; and when the vote of the war-archon was given to them that counseled battle, it was agreed that battle should be given. After this, each one of those generals that had given his vote for joining battle, when his turn of command came round—for each man commanded in turn day by day—gave up his turn to Miltiades. Nevertheless Miltiades made not use of any of their turns, but waited till his own proper turn came round. And when this was come then the Athenians were drawn up in order of battle; their right wing was led by Callimachus—for in those days it was the custom among the Athenians that the war-archon should lead the right wing—and after him came the tribes of the Athenians, one after the other, in their order, according to their numbers, and last of all, upon the left wing, were the men of Platæa. And ever since the battle that was fought upon this day it has been the custom among the Athenians, when they hold their sacrifice and solemn convocation in the fifth year, that the herald of the Athenians should pray aloud in these words: "May the Gods send all blessings to the men of Athens and to the men of Platæa." Now the Athenians sought to make their line of battle equal to the line of the Persians; and that they might do so they took away men from the center, so that this was the weakest part of the army, the wings being the strongest. And so, so soon as the battle had been set in array, and the sacrifice being made appeared to be favorable, then the Athenians, being let go, charged the Persians at a running pace, the space between the two armies being eight furlongs or thereabouts. And the Persians, when they saw them coming against them at a run, made ready to receive them, but thought that they must be possessed with utter madness and frenzy, seeing that they were so few in number and yet were running to meet them, and this though they had neither horsemen nor archers. So the barbarians judged; but not the less the Athenians, joining battle in one body with their enemies, quitted themselves in a manner worthy of all praise. For indeed never before had Greeks so charged against their enemies in battle at a running pace, nor had any before endured to see without fear men clad and armed in the fashion of the Medes. For indeed before that day the very name of the Medes had been a terror to the Greeks to hear. Long time did the barbarians and Athenians fight together in Marathon. In the middle of the line the barbarians prevailed, for there the Persians and the Sacæ had their place. These broke the line of the Greeks, and pursued them for some space toward the mountains. But on each of the two wings the Greeks prevailed, the Athenians being on the one wing and the men of Platæa upon the other. These, having broken their enemies, suffered them to flee, and then wheeling round the two wings upon the barbarians that had broken the middle of the line, they prevailed over these also. Then the Persians fled to their ships, and the Athenians pursued them, smiting them and slaying them; and when they, pursuing them, came to the sea, they called for fire and would have burned the ships. In this part of the battle fell Callimachus, the war-archon, who had shown himself that day a man of valor. Also there fell Stesilaus, son of Thrasilaus, being one of the ten generals. Also Cynægirus, son to Euphorion, whose brother was Æschylus the poet, was slain at this time; for, laying hold of the stern ornament of one of the ships of the Persians, he had his hand cut off by the blow of an ax; and there perished with him other Athenians also of note and name. Nevertheless the Athenians took seven of the ships at this time. With the rest the barbarians pushed off from the shore, and having taken up the prisoners from Eretria from the island whereon they had left them, they sailed round the promontory of Sunium, hoping that they should come to the city before that the army of the Athenians should be able to return thither. In this matter the house of the sons of Alcmæon were accused by their fellow countrymen, who said that they had held up a shield for a signal to the Persians; and that it had been covenanted that they should do so, that the Persians might take the city unawares and empty of men. So the Persians sailed round Cape Sunium; and the Athenians marched with all the speed that they could that they might defend the city; and when they were come they encamped in the precinct of Hercules, that is at Cynosargæ; and it so chanced that they came from the precinct of Hercules that is in Marathon. For a while the ships of the barbarians lay off Phalerum, which was in those days the port of Athens, but in no long time sailed back to Asia.

MARATHON

In this battle that was fought at Marathon there were slain of the barbarians six thousand and four hundred or thereabouts, and of the Athenians one hundred and ninety and two. In the battle also there happened this marvel. A man of Athens, Epizelus by name, the son of Couphagoras, fighting in the press, and bearing himself bravely, was of a sudden smitten with blindness, and this without being wounded any where in the body or stricken at all. And he was blind for the remainder of his days. Now the story which this man told about the matter was this. "I saw," he said, "a man of great stature fully armed stand over against me, and he had a great beard that covered his whole shield. Me indeed he passed by, but the man that stood next to me he smote and slew."

When Datis was on his way to Asia, being at Myconos, he saw a vision in his sleep. What this vision was no man knows; but this is certain that so soon as the day dawned he caused a search to be made in all the ships; and in a certain Phœnician ship he found an image of Apollo that was covered with gold, and would know whence it had been brought. And when he knew from what temple it had been taken, he sailed with his own ship to Delos. And he put the image in the temple and laid a command upon the men of Delos—for they had by this time come back to their island—that they should carry back the image to the Delian temple of the Thebans. (This temple stands on the sea shore over against Chalcis.) When he had given these commands Datis departed, but the men of Delos neglected to do as he had said; but twenty years after the Thebans, having been warned by an oracle, fetched it themselves.

When Datis and Artaphernes were come to Asia they took the people of Eretria whom they had carried away captive and brought them up to Susa, to King Darius. Now King Darius had before this been greatly enraged against the people of Eretria, holding that they had done him wrong without provocation; but when he saw them thus brought before him and in his power, he did them no harm, but settled them in a station of his own in the land of the Cissia. This station was called Ardericca, and it is distant from Susa twenty and six miles or thereabouts. Five miles from this Ardericca is a great well whence they got three things, to wit, bitumen, salt, and oil. Here then King Darius settled the people of Eretria, and here they remained many years afterwards still speaking their own language.

When the full moon was past there came to Athens two thousand Lacedæmonians, having marched with all speed, so that they came to Athens on the third day after they had set out from Sparta. These, though they had come too late for the battle; much desired to see the Persians that had been slain. So they went to Marathon, and when they had seen them and had greatly praised the Athenians and their valor, they departed to their own home.

CHAPTER V

OF THE SONS OF ALCMÆON AND THE END OF MILTIADES

THIS story that they tell of the sons of Alcmæon, how they held up a shield to the Persians seeking to destroy the city, that it might be under the lordship of Hippias, is passing strange, seeing that the house of Alcmæon had showed itself an enemy to tyrants not less than any other house among the Greeks. And indeed so long as the lordship of the sons of Pisistratus endured at Athens, so long did they remain in exile; and as for the ending of this lordship, they are to be praised for it rather than are Harmodius and Aristogeiton, for these did but make the sons of Pisistratus the more cruel by slaying Hipparchus; but as for making their tyranny to cease they did nothing. This was the work of the sons of Alcmæon if it be true, as has been told, that they had persuaded the Pythia for money to lay this charge upon the Lacedæmonians that they should cause Athens to be free. Nor indeed is it to be thought that the sons of Alcmæon betrayed their country by reason of anger against their countrymen; for there were none in those days of greater reputation than were these men, nor any that were more honored. That a shield was held up is certain; but as to who it was that held it up, this no man knows.

THE RACE IN ARMOUR

As for the house of Alcmæon it was famous in Athens from the beginning; but there were two men that more than all others made it to be of great renown; and these two were Alcmæon and Megacles. As for Alcmæon, how he got him great riches from Crœsus, King of Lydia, has been told already; and as for Megacles the matter stands thus.

Cleisthenes son of Aristonymus, being lord of Sicyon, would have for his daughter's husband that man whom he should find to be noblest of all the Greeks. The name of this daughter was Agarista. For this purpose he caused proclamation to be made at the festival of Olympia, where he had won a victory with a chariot of four horses. And the proclamation was this: "Let any Greek who holds himself to be worthy of being son-in-law to Cleisthenes come on the sixtieth day, or before it if he will, to the city of Sicyon, for Cleisthenes will determine in the space of a year, beginning with the sixtieth day, to whom he should give his daughter in marriage." To Cleisthenes therefore came so many of the Greeks as thought much of themselves or of their house; and he had prepared a course for foot-racing and a wrestling ground to make trial of them. From Italy came Smindyrides of Sybaris, that was the most luxurious liver of all the men of his day. And those were the times when the city of Sybaris was at the very height of its prosperity. And from Ætolia there came Males brother of Titormus. This Titormus excelled all men in strength. He it was that seeking to withdraw himself altogether from the sight of men fled into the furthest parts of Ætolia. There came also Leocedes, son of Pheidon, that was lord of Argos. This was that Pheidon who brought in the weights and measures that the dwellers in Peloponnese use. No man was more arrogant than he. He drove out the men of Elis from being masters of the festivals of Olympia and was master himself. Also among the suitors was Laphanes the Arcadian, the son of Euphorion, who, so say the Arcadians, received in his house the Twin-Brethren, and ever after used hospitality to all comers. From Athens there came Hippoclides, the son of Tisander, who excelled all the Athenians in riches and beauty; and also Megacles, being son to that Alcmæon whom King Crœsus had made rich. These and others also came to Sicyon as suitors for Agarista on the sixtieth day, as had been appointed. Then Cleisthenes first of all inquired of each his country and his father's house; and afterwards, for the space of a whole year, made trial of their courage and their temper and their training and their behavior, having converse with them sometimes one by one and sometimes altogether. Such as were younger among them he would send to the place of games; but chiefly he made trial of all at the banqueting table. Thus he behaved himself with them for the space of a whole year entertaining them right splendidly the whole year. And of all the suitors none pleased him so well as the two that came from Athens, and of these two he inclined the rather to Hippoclides, not only for his high carriage, but also because he was of kin to the house of Cypselus that had had the lordship of Corinth.

THE BANQUETING TABLE

When the day came for the espousals, and for Cleisthenes to declare his mind whom he chose out of the suitors for his daughter's husband, he sacrificed a hundred oxen and made a great feast to the suitors and to all the people of Sicyon. And after the feast the suitors contended with each other in music and in speaking on some subject that was proposed to them. And as the drinking went on, Hippoclides, all the others wondering much at him, bade the flute-player play music to him; and when the flute-player did so, he danced. And in this dancing he pleased himself marvelously, but Cleisthenes looked askance on the whole business. Again, after resting awhile, Hippoclides bade them bring a table; and when the table was brought, he mounted upon it, and danced, first certain Spartan figures, and then certain Athenian; and at the last, with his head upon the table, he began to toss his legs about in the air. During the first dancing, and during the second, Cleisthenes held his peace, not with wishing to break out upon the man, though indeed he loathed to think of having Hippoclides for a son-in-law, so much did he hate the man's passion for dancing and his shamelessness. But when he saw him tossing his legs in the air he could restrain himself no longer, but cried aloud: "Son of Tisander, thou hast danced away thy wife!" And the young man said: "Hippoclides does not care!" which words have become a proverb among the Greeks. After this Cleisthenes commanded silence, and spake thus in the midst of the suitors: "My friends that are come to be suitors of my daughter, I am well pleased with all of you, and gladly would I content you all, if it were possible, and not choose out one from among you and reject the rest. But this, seeing that I have to dispose of a single maiden in marriage, I cannot do. To you therefore who are disappointed in your suit I give a gift, a talent of silver to each man, because ye have done me honor in seeking to take a wife from my house, and because ye have been at charge, living away from your homes. But my daughter Agarista I betroth to Megacles, the son

of Alcmæon, after the custom of the land of Attica."
And when Megacles had also plighted his troth, the
marriage was made. Thus did the house of Alcmæon
become famous throughout the land of Greece. To these
two, Megacles and Agarista, was born Cleisthenes, the
same that divided the Athenians into tribes and set up
also the rule of the people. This name he had from his
grandfather of Sicyon. Also there was born another
son, Hippocrates, and Hippocrates had a son Megacles
and a daughter Agarista. This Agarista was married to
Xanthippus the son of Ariphon; and being with child,
she had a vision in her sleep, and dreamed that she
brought forth a lion. Not many days afterwards she
bore a son whose name was Pericles.

Now shall be told the end of Miltiades. This man,
after the battle that was fought at Marathon, having
been held before in high esteem among his countrymen,
increased yet more in reputation. This being so, he
asked of the Athenians seventy ships and an army and
money. He told them not to what place he purposed to
take the ships, saying only that if they would hearken
to him he would greatly enrich them; for he would
take them to a land whence they might easily get gold
without stint. In this way he asked for the ships, and the
Athenians, being carried away by what they heard, gave
him that which he asked for. Then Miltiades, having
got the ships and the army, sailed to the island of Paros.
And the cause which he pretended for so doing was
that the Parians had first made war against Athens,
for that they had sent a ship of war with the Persians.
This cause indeed he pretended; but in truth he had a

grudge against a certain man of Paros, Lysagoras by name, because he had slandered him to Hydarnes the Persian. When Miltiades was come to Paros, the Parians took refuge within their walls; and a siege was begun. Then he sent a herald to the city, and demanded of the Parians a hundred talents, saying that he would not take his army thence till he had destroyed them, if they would not pay the money. Now the Parians had no thought of paying the money to Miltiades; but they did their utmost to strengthen their city against him, contriving many devices, among which was this, that where the wall was weakest there they built it up to twice the height that it had before.

So far in the story are the Greeks agreed. But what happened after this is thus told by the men of Paros. To Miltiades, being in great straits, there came a woman that was a priestess, a Parian by birth, whose name was Timo; and she was a priestess of the lower gods, but one of the meaner sort. This woman came to Miltiades and said to him: "If thou hast set thy mind on taking Paros, do what I shall tell thee and thou shalt have thy wish." And when she had unfolded to him her counsel, he went to the hill that is before the city and leaped over the fence that is about the precinct of Demeter the Lawgiver, for the door he was not able to open. And after leaping over the fence, he went to the sanctuary; and what he purposed to do therein, whether to move any of the things that may not be touched, or any other thing, no man can say; but when he was come to the door there fell suddenly upon him a great horror, so that he went back by the way by which he had come.

But as he leaped over the fence he strained his thigh, or, as some say, he bruised his knee upon the ground.

After this Miltiades, being in evil case, went back to Athens, but he brought the people no money, neither had he conquered Paros for them. Only he had besieged the city for twenty and six days, and had laid waste the island. And when the men of Paros knew of the priestess, that she had led Miltiades into the temple, so soon as the siege was at an end they sent worshipers to Delphi who should inquire whether they should not slay the priestess that had meditated the betraying of the country, and had caused Miltiades to see the holy things which it is not lawful for any man to behold. But the Pythia answered: "Slay her not; for it was the will of the Gods that Miltiades should come to an evil end, and this woman led him unto the same." As for Miltiades, when he was come back to Athens the Athenians had much talk about him; and the chief of his enemies was Xanthippus. This man brought him to trial for his life before the people, whom, he said, he had deceived. And Miltiades, though he was present at his trial, could not plead for himself because his thigh was sorely diseased, but lay there upon a couch, while his friends pleaded earnestly on his behalf, saying much about the battle of Marathon and how he had taken the island of Lemnos. And the favor of the people was with him, so that they did not take away his life; yet was he condemned for his wrong-doing in a fine of fifty talents. After this Miltiades died in his prison, for the bone of his thigh had splintered, and the flesh was mortified. And the fine was paid by Cimon his son.

CHAPTER VI

HOW PREPARATION WAS MADE FOR THE SECOND WAR AGAINST THE GREEKS

WHEN King Darius heard tidings of the battle at Marathon, his wrath, which was already hot against the Athenians by reason of their doings at Sardis, waxed yet more fierce, so that he was more earnest than ever to make war against Greece. And straightway he sent messengers to all the cities in his dominions, bidding them gather together soldiers—and of these many more than he had commanded before—and with these, ships and horsemen and food and vessels of transport. And for the space of three years after these commands had been given, all Asia was in an uproar, seeing that the bravest of her children were being chosen to march against the Greeks, and were making ready to go. But in the fourth year the Egyptians, who had been enslaved by Cambyses revolted. Then was Darius more zealous than before to march both against the Athenians and the Egyptians. But while he was making ready so to do, there came a great disputing among his sons who should be King after him; for the law of the Persians is that the King declares who shall reign after him before he goes to the war. Now Darius had had three sons born to him by his wife the daughter of Gobryas; and these were born before that he was made King: and after that he was made King he had four others born to him of Atossa that was the daughter of Cyrus. Of the first three Artabazanes was the eldest, and of the four Xerxes. These disputed among themselves, and Artabazanes claimed the kingdom because he was the eldest of all, and because it was the custom over all the world that the eldest should have the pre-eminence; but Xerxes claimed it because his mother was daughter to Cyrus, and it was Cyrus that had established the kingdom of the Persians. Now while Darius doubted about the matter, there came up to Susa Demaratus the son of Ariston. The same had been deprived of his kingdom in Sparta and had fled from the city. When this man knew what it was that the sons of Darius disputed about, he came forward, according to report, and gave counsel to Xerxes that over and above the words that he had said he should say also this, that he had been born when Darius was already King and had dominion over all the Persians, but that Darius was a subject only when Artabazanes was born. "And indeed at Sparta," said Demaratus, "the law is this, that if a king have children that are born before he be made King, and also a child that is born after, then he that is born after is preferred." Of these words of Demaratus Xerxes made such use that King Darius declared that he should be King in his room. But in the year after it so befell that while he was preparing to make war both against the Greeks and against the Egyptians, King Darius died, having reigned over the Persians thirty and six years in all; and Xerxes his son reigned in his stead. Now at the first Xerxes by no means desired to make war against the Greeks, but against the Egyptians he made great preparations. Then said Mardonius the son of Gobryas, who was cousin to the King, being sister's son to King Darius, "My lord, it is by no means fitting that the Athenians, seeing that they have done grievous wrong to the Persians, should thus go unpunished. Do therefore first the thing that thou hast now in hand, and when thou hast humbled the Egyptians go forth against the Greeks. So shalt thou have great renown throughout the world, and men shall fear hereafter to trouble thy land." And besides thus speaking of vengeance, Mardonius would also add that Europe was a very beautiful land, bearing all manner of fruitful trees, and of an excellent fertility, and altogether such that no man but the King was worthy to possess it. All this he said because he was a lover of change and adventure; also he hoped to be made ruler over the land of Greece. And at last he had his way, persuading Xerxes to take the matter in hand. There were other things that helped him persuading Xerxes to this act. First there came envoys from the house of Aleuas, that was King in Thessaly, who would fain have the King come against the land of Greece, and showed all zeal in his cause. Also certain of the house of Pisistratus that had come up to Susa held the same language. These had with them one Onomacritus, a man of Athens, that was a soothsayer, and one that had set in order the prophecies of Musæus. Once, indeed, there had been enmity between the son of Pisistratus and this Onomacritus; for Hipparchus had banished him from Athens, having found that he had added to the prophecies of Musæus a certain prophecy how that an island which lies near unto Lemnos should one day be swallowed up in the sea. A certain Leros had found him out in this, and Hipparchus banished him, having been wont to consult him continually. But now the sons of Pisistratus were reconciled to him, and took him in their company to Susa, and talked much of him and of his wisdom. And so soon as he was brought before the King, he repeated to him certain of the prophecies. If there were any prophecy that spake of disaster to the Persians, of this he would make no mention, but such as seemed to promise them success he would set forth, how that it was in the fates that a Persian should bridge over the Hellespont. Thus did Onomacritus make much of his prophecies, and the sons of Pisistratus and the sons of Aleuas set forth their opinions to the same purpose.

So King Xerxes was persuaded to make war upon the Greeks. And first, in the second year after the death of Darius, he marched into the land of Egypt, and having enslaved it more than it had been enslaved before, he gave it over to Achæmenes his brother, and son to Darius. (This Achæmenes was afterward slain by Inaros, the son of Psammeticus, a Nubian.) And after this, being now about to lead his army against Athens, he called an assembly of the noblest of the Persians, that he might hear what they thought, and might himself say what he would have them hear. And when they were gathered together he spake, saying, "There is a custom, which, indeed, I did not first establish, but received it from the kings before me, that we Persians have never rested since the day when we took this kingdom from the Medes. So the Gods will have it and in so doing have we greatly prospered. What nations Cyrus and Cambyses and Darius my father subdued ye know well. And since I came to this kingdom I have studied how I might show myself to be not behind them, and might not the less increase our Empire. And now I will set before you what I purpose. I will bridge over the Hellespont and cross into Europe that I may avenge my father and this nation upon the Athenians for all the wrong that they have done, burning their city with fire. Nor shall we get vengeance only, but this good also, that conquering the Athenians and their neighbors that dwell in the island of Pelops, we shall have the whole earth subject to us, for I take it that when these Greeks have been subdued there is no city or nation that shall be able to stand against us. This then is my judgment, but I would have you say what is in your minds. Speak, therefore."

THE COUNCIL

Then spake Mardonius: "O my lord, thou showest thyself to be the noblest of the Persians, not of those only that have been in former times, but also of all that shall be hereafter, when thou settest forth such good counsels in such excellent words. Surely it is not well that these men of Ionia should laugh at us and go unpunished, and that when we have subdued Indians and Assyrians and Ethiopians, not because they had done us wrong, but because we would enlarge our borders, we should leave these Greeks unharmed after that they have done us wrongs grievous and many. And that we may easily vanquish them, I doubt not at all. For I myself, at the bidding of my father Darius, marched against them, and went so far as the land of Macedonia, and indeed had come to the city of Athens itself, nor did I find any that dared meet me in battle. And yet, as I hear, these Greeks are wont to fight in a most foolish and ignorant fashion. For when they have declared war against one another, then they choose out the fairest and smoothest plot that they can find, and come down to this, and so fight that they who have the better in the battle yet depart not without great loss; as for them that are worsted there is nothing to be said, for they are utterly destroyed. For why, seeing that they are all of them one language, do they not send heralds and messengers, and so compose their differences peaceably, rather than settle them by fighting? And, if they must needs fight, why do they not make the best each of them of that which they have, and so join in battle? And yet, notwithstanding this their folly, when I marched so far as Macedonia, not one of them dared to meet me.

And now, O King, who will stand up against thee when thou bringest with thee all the warriors out of the land of Asia and the ships also? And if they be so mad as to stand, then shall they learn that we Persians are the greatest warriors on the face of the earth."

When Mardonius had thus spoken all the other Persians kept silence; but at the last Artabanus, the son of Hystaspes, being uncle to King Xerxes, and so taking courage to speak, put forth a contrary opinion in these words: "O King, if there be not set forth opinions that are contrary the one to the other, thou canst not choose the better, but must follow the one which thou hearest. For it is with opinions as it is with gold. Pure gold we know not so long as it is left by itself, but when we rub it against that which is not pure, then we know it. I counseled thy father Darius that he should not make war on the Scythians, men that have no city to dwell in; but he, thinking to subdue them, would not hearken to me, but marched against them, and lost many and brave soldiers. And now thou hast it in thy heart to make war against men that are far better than the Scythians, being mighty both by sea and land. Hear, therefore, into what danger thou art moving. Thou wilt bridge over the Hellespont, and march into the land of Greece. Suppose that thou suffer defeat, whether it be by sea or by land, or, haply, by both, for the men are valiant (and, indeed, what they can do we know full well, for Datis and Artaphernes, when they led a mighty host into Attica, the Athenians alone defeated). But suppose they get the mastery by sea only, and so, sailing to the Hellespont, break down the bridge. This surely, O

King, would be a terrible thing. Nor is this thing that I say of my own devising. For thy father Darius bridged over the Thracian Bosphorus and the Danube, and so marched against the Scythians. And when the Scythians used all manner of entreaties to the Ionians, to whom indeed the King had entrusted the charge of the bridge, if Histiæus of Miletus had followed the judgment of the other lords of the Ionians in this and had set himself against us, then had the power of the Persians been utterly destroyed. Surely it is a dreadful thing even to speak of, that the fortunes of the King should have rested upon the will of one man. Put away, therefore, O King, I beseech thee, this thy purpose to run without any need into this great danger, and hearken unto me. Break up this council and think over this matter in thine heart, and afterward declare unto us thy purpose, and remember this also, that God smites with his thunder such creatures as are tall and strong, passing by them that are smaller and weaker, and that it is on the tallest houses and trees that his bolts for the most part fall. For he is wont to bring down all high things. So otherwise a very great host is often put to flight by a few men, God sending upon it some storm or panic, for he will not suffer any but himself to have high thoughts. And as to thee, Mardonius, thou doest ill, speaking lightly against the Greeks, and persuading the King to head his army against them; for this thou manifestly wishest. God grant that thou succeed not in thy purpose. But if it must needs be that we march against the Greeks, then at the least let the King remain here safe at home. And let us make this wager between ourselves. Choose out for thyself such men as thou wilt have, and take with thee an army so great as thou desirest, and if things go as thou sayest that they will, according to the pleasure of the King, then let my children be slain, and I also with them. But if things go not so, then shall thy children be slain, and thou also with them, if indeed thou shalt ever come back. But if thou shalt not take this wager, and wilt still march against the Greeks, then am I sure that they who are left in this land will hear that Mardonius has perished, having first worked great harm to the Persians, and lies torn by dogs and birds in the land of the Athenians, or, it may be, of the Lacedæmonians, having so learned what manner of men they are against whom thou persuadest the King to make war."

When Artabanus had thus spoken, Xerxes was very wroth, and cried, "Artabanus, thou art brother to my father, and this kinship shall save thee, so that thou shalt not receive the due reward of thy folly. Nevertheless, this disgrace I ordain for thee, for thy evil-mindedness and cowardice; thou shalt not march with me against this land of Greece, but shalt remain here with the women, and I without thee will accomplish that I have said. For let me not be said to be the son of Darius, the son of Hystaspes, the son of Arsemes, the son of Ariaramness, the son of Teispes, the son of Cyrus, the son of Cambyses, the son of Teispes, the son of Achæmenes, if I avenge not myself on these Athenians. Verily I believe that if I do not so they will come against this land, so bold have they shown themselves in time past, so that if we subdue them not, then will they subdue us, for indeed there is nothing between these two things. Rightly then shall I make war against these men, and so learn what is this great danger that lies in dealing with them, for are they not the same whom Pelops the Phrygian, that was servant to the kings my fathers, subdued so utterly, that their land is called the Island of Pelops to this day?"

But when it was night the King was much troubled by the words of Artabanus; and taking counsel with himself, he judged that it would not be well to make war against the Greeks, and so fell asleep. But in the night, so say the Persians, he saw a vision. There stood over him a man tall and fair, who spake to him, saying, "Man of Persia, dost thou then change thy purpose so that after bidding the Persians gather together a great army, now thou wilt not lead it against the Greeks? Thou dost not well so to change. Go rather on the way whereon thou hast set out." When the man had said so much he vanished out of the King's sight. But when the day dawned Xerxes made no account of the vision that he had seen, but called together the Persians, as he had done the day before, and spake to them, saying, "Forgive me, men of Persia, if I change the purpose that I had yesterday; for I am not yet grown to the full height of my understanding, and they that give me this counsel cease not urging me. When therefore I heard the words of Artabanus the spirit of youth grew hot within me, and I spake to him such words as I should not have spoken, seeing that he is an old man. But now I confess my fault and yield myself to his judgment. Rest therefore in peace, knowing that I have changed my purpose, and will not make war against the Greeks."

When the Persians heard these words they rejoiced

greatly and worshiped the King. But when it was night there came again the same vision to Xerxes, and stood over him, and spake, saying, "Son of Darius, thou hast declared thyself openly before all the Persians, changing thy purpose about this expedition, and taking no account of my words. Know this, therefore, that if thou do not go straightway on this journey, there shall rise out of the matter this ending, As thou didst become in a short space great and the lord of many men, so shalt thou in a short space be brought low."

When Xerxes heard these words he was much dismayed, and leaped up from his bed and sent a messenger to call Artabanus. And when he was come, Xerxes said to him, "Artabanus, I was not well advised, speaking to thee unseemly words when thou hadst given me good counsel. But in a short time I repented me purposing to do the things which thou didst counsel me. But though this is my purpose, I am not able to follow it; for now that I am changed and have repented of my folly, there appears to me a vision haunting me, and in nowise consenting to my resolve. And even now it has threatened me and departed. If therefore it be God that sends this vision to me, and if it be altogether according to his will that I should make this expedition against Greece, then the same vision will come to thee, and command thee the same things that it commanded me. And this, I think, will most surely happen if thou wilt take all my royal apparel and put it on thee, and so sit on my seat, and afterward sleep in my bed.

This at the first Artabanus was loth to do, but at the last moment consented to it. But first he spake to the

King, saying, "When thou didst reproach me, O King, this troubled me not, but rather to see that when there were set before the Persians two counsels, whereof the one tended to increase their pride, and the other to prudence, thou didst choose the worse. And now that thou hast turned to wiser counsels thou sayest that there came a vision that will not suffer thee to cease from this purpose of war, and that it comes by the sending of a god. Now as to dreams and visions, know that there is nothing divine in them, but that they wander about at random. For I am much older than thou, and know more of such things. Now men are wont to dream of such things as they have been concerned with in the day; and we have been much concerned with this matter of the war. But if this vision be not such as I think, but rather as thou sayest, of the sending of a god, then will it appear and lay its commands upon me even as it did upon thee; nor should it appear to me at all the more because I wear thy clothing or sit upon thy seat. For this thing, whatever it be, that thou seest in thy dreams can not be so foolish as to think that I am thou, because I wear thy clothing. Now if it takes no heed of me, and still appear to thee saying the same things, then shall I myself judge it to be of God. For the rest, if it be thy purpose that I wear thy apparel, and sleep in thy bed, be it so; let the vision appear to me. But for the present I hold to my own opinion."

So much said Artabanus, hoping to persuade Xerxes that the thing was naught. He put on the King's apparel, and sat on his throne, and afterward lay down to sleep in his bed. And when he was asleep there came to him the same vision that had come to Xerxes, and stood over him and spake, saying, "Thou art he that persuadeth Xerxes not to make war against the Greeks, having, thou sayest, a care for him. Verily thou shalt not go unpunished, either now or hereafter, seeking to hinder that which it is the purpose of God to bring to pass. And as for what Xerxes shall suffer if he be disobedient in this matter, it has been declared to him already."

When the vision had thus spoken it seemed to Artabanus to make as if it were about to burn out his eyes with hot irons. Then he cried aloud, and leaped up from the bed, and sat him down by Xerxes and told him all that he had seen. And afterward he said to the King, 'I am one, O King, that has seen strong things overthrown by the weak, and so I would not have thee yield to thy desires, knowing that it was an evil thing to covet great possessions, and remembering how ill Cyrus fared when he made war against the Massagetæ, and Cambyses against the Ethiopians, and having myself gone with Darius against the Scythians. But now since this inspiration comes from God, who is preparing, it seems, utter destruction against the Greeks, I change my counsel. Do thou therefore declare to the Persians the purpose of God, and take good care that if God give thee this opportunity, thou shalt not fail any thing on thy part."

So soon therefore as it was day Xerxes told the whole matter to the Persians, and Artabanus, who had been the only one to speak against the war, was now the foremost in urging it.

CHAPTER VII

OF THE SETTING FORTH OF XERXES

For the space of four years from the subduing of Egypt did the servants of King Xerxes gather together the host and all such things as were needful for it. And in the beginning of the fifth year the King set out upon his march, having such an army as had never before been seen. For indeed that which Darius led against the Scythians was as nothing in comparison of this, neither was that wherewith the Scythians invaded the land of Asia, and subdued the northern parts thereof (this was the cause why Darius invaded the land of the Scythians), nor that which the sons of Atreus led against Troy, nor that of the Mysians and Teucrians, who, in the days before the Trojan war, conquered the land of Thrace, and came as far as the river Peneus that is in the land of Thessaly. Not one of these armies is worthy to be compared with the army of Xerxes. For what people of Asia did he not lead against Greece? And what stream, saving only the great rivers, was not drunk up by his armies? Some were bidden to furnish foot soldiers, and some horsemen, and some ships for carrying of horses and men at arms, and some ships of war for the bridges, and others food and ships. First of all, seeing that they who had first sailed against Greece had suffered great loss at Mount Athos, Xerxes caused that there should be a fleet of ships of war at Elæus, and that men from the ships, taking turn by turn, should dig a great trench, digging under the lash of taskmasters, in which work the people of the country also took their part.

Now this Athos is a great and famous mountain, that stretches out into the sea, and the land by which it is joined to the continent is narrow, being of the breadth of a mile and a half. Across this Xerxes would have them dig a trench. And the men dug it after this fashion. A line was drawn across by the city Sane, and the nations divided the work among themselves. When the trench was now deep, some stood below and dug, and others handed up the earth to men that stood on ladders, and these again to others, till it was brought to the top, and so carried away. The greater part had double trouble with the digging, the sides breaking away continually; nor indeed could it have been otherwise, seeing that they made the measure of the top and the measure of the bottom to be the same. But with the Phœnicians it was not so, for they showed their wisdom in this as they commonly do in other things. When they had had their part allotted to them, they made their digging at the top twice as broad as was needed for the trench; but as they went down they made it narrower, till at the bottom it was of the same width as the rest. Near to the trench was a plain, wherein there was a market and a place for buying and selling; and much corn, ready ground, was brought to the place from Asia.

This work, it would seem, Xerxes did from pride, wishing to show his might, and to leave a memorial of himself. For when he might without trouble have had his ships drawn across the isthmus, he commanded that a trench should be made from one sea to the other, and this of such a breadth that two ships of war could pass. And he also commanded them that had the business of digging this trench that they should build a bridge over the river Strymon. Other preparations also were made, ropes of papyrus and of white flax for the bridges, and stores of food for the army and for the beasts of burden.

The place of gathering for the armies was Critalla in Cappadocia. Setting out thence, it marched through the land of Phrygia to the city of Celænæ, which is on the river Mæander. Here in the market-place is hung out the skin of Marsyas the Satyr, whom Apollo flayed, when he had vanquished him in a conquest of singing.

In this city there dwelt a certain Pythius, the son of Atys, a Lydian. This man entertained Xerxes and his whole army with very great hospitality, and said also that he was willing to give him money for the war. And when the King heard this talk of money, he asked them that stood by, saying, "Who is this Pythius, and what wealth has he that he makes such promises?" And they said, "O King, this is the man that gave the golden plane-tree to King Darius thy father, and the vine also; and he surpasses all men there are in wealth, thou only being excepted, O King." At the last words Xerxes marveled much; and he called Pythius and asked him, saying, "What is the sum of thy wealth?" And Pythius made answer, "I will hide nothing from thee, nor will I make any pretense that I do not know the sum of my substance. I know it, and will declare it truly to you. So soon as I knew that you were purposing to come down with your army to the sea of the Greeks, because I wished to furnish you with some money for the war, I reckoned up all that belongs to me, and found that I have two thousand talents of silver and four millions of gold darics, wanting seven thousand only. All this I willingly give thee for a gift; and I shall still have sufficient from my fields and from my slaves."

These words pleased King Xerxes much, and he said, "Since I came out from the land Persia I have not found a man who was willing to give entertainment to my whole army, and also to furnish money for the war, saving thee only. But thou hast entertained my army in royal fashion, and now makest offer of much money. Now for all this I will make thee this return. First of all thou shalt be my friend from this time forth, and thy four millions of darics I will complete out of my own treasury, giving thee the seven thousand that thou lackest, that the tale may be completed. Do thou therefore keep for thyself that which thou hast gained. And remember to be such always as thou hast shown thyself to-day, for he that doeth such things will in no wise repent himself of them either now or in the time to come."

When he had said this, and had made good his promises, he went on his way. And he came to Colossæ, a great city of Phrygia, where the river Lycus entering a great gulf flows for five furlongs under the earth, and from Colossæ to Cydrara, where King Crœsus had set up a pillar to mark the boundaries of Lydia. After this he saw a plane-tree which was so fair that for the sake of its beauty he gave it ornaments of gold, and appointed one of the Immortals to have the charge of it. So he came to the city of Sardis.

Being arrived at this city he straightway sent heralds to Greece who should ask for earth and water, as tokens that they gave themselves and their country to the King. To Athens, indeed, and to Sparta he sent not, but to all other cities he sent, for he thought that they who had refused to give them on the sending of King Darius would now give them for fear of his host.

Now the cause why he sent not heralds to Athens and Sparta was this, that these cities had dealt evilly with the heralds which King Darius had sent on this errand, the Athenians throwing them down into the pit, which is the place of punishment for such as are appointed to die, and the Spartans casting them into a well and bidding them take earth and water for themselves. What ill thing befell the Athenians by reason of their having dealt so unrighteously with the heralds it is not possible to discern, unless indeed it be that their city and country were laid waste; but for this laying waste there was doubtless another cause. But on the Spartans there came trouble from the wrath of Talthybius, the same that was herald to King Agamemnon. (There is a temple of this Talthybius in Sparta, and when there is any sending of heralds from Sparta, his descendants, who are called the sons of Talthybius, are sent.) After the doing of this deed the Spartans found no good tokens in their sacrifices. And when this had been so for many days, the Spartans were much troubled, and called many assemblies of the people about this matter. At the last they made proclamation inquiring whether any Spartan were willing to die for his country. Whereupon two men, Sperthias the son of Aneristus, and Bulis the son of Nicolaus, nobles both of them, and than whom there were none more wealthy in Sparta, of their own free-will offered themselves as an offering of atonement to Xerxes, and the Spartans sent them to the Persians as men that were doomed to die. In their journey to Susa they came to Hydarnes. This Hydarnes was a Persian, and governor of all them that dwelt on the sea-coast of Asia. This man showed them hospitality; and as they sat at the banquet, he said to them, "Men of Sparta, why are you not willing to be friends with the King? Ye see that the King knows how to honor good men, for consider me and my fortune. And ye also, if you would give yourselves to the King—for the King knows that ye are good men—would be rulers of the land of Greece by the King's favor." To this the men answered, "Thy counsel, Hydarnes, is not the counsel of one that knows the whole matter. Thou knowest indeed what it is to be a slave, but of freedom thou hast never made trial, whether it be sweet or no. Surely if thou hadst made such trial thou wouldst counsel us to fight for it, not with the spear only, but also with the battle-ax."

Such was the answer which the men made to Hydarnes. After this they went unto Susa, and came before the King. And when the guards would have had them fall down before the King and do obeisance, these two Spartans refused. "We will not do it," said they; "no, not if ye thrust our heads down to the ground, for it is not our custom to fall down before any man, neither are we come hither for any such thing." In this manner they escaped the doing such obeisance. Afterward they spake to the King, saying, "King of the Medes, the Lacedæmonians have sent us to make atonement for thy heralds that were slain in Sparta." But Xerxes, for greatness of heart, would not take such atonement. "The Spartans," he said, "when they do such things overthrow all law and justice among men; but I will not make myself like unto them. I will neither do the thing for the doing of which I reproach them, nor will I loose them from their guilt by slaying the men that they have sent to me."

By these means the anger of Talthybius was staid awhile, and this though Sperthias and Bulis came back safe to Sparta. Nevertheless many years afterward it fell on the Spartans, as they themselves say, in the great war that was waged between them and the Athenians. That this wrath should fall on envoys of the Spartans, and should not cease till it was satisfied, seems to be just; but that the men on whom it fell should be children of these same two that were sent to the King at Susa, this is passing strange. Yet so it fell out. For Nicolaüs the son of Bulis, and Aneristus the son of Sperthias, having been sent as ambassadors to Asia, were betrayed by Sitalces, King of Thrace, to the Athenians, and being carried to Attica, there perished, and with them Aristeas of Corinth. These things came to pass many years after the expedition of King Xerxes.

When the messengers, then, had been sent to the cities of the Greeks, the King prepared to march to Abydos, purposing to pass over thence into Europe.

CHAPTER VIII

OF THE MARCH OF XERXES

WHILE Xerxes tarried at Sardis, they that were appointed to this business made a bridge over the Hellespont, from Abydos to a certain rocky land that runs out into the sea on the other side, the space between being seven furlongs. One line the Phœnicians made with cables of white flax, and the other the Egyptians, with cables of papyrus. But when the work was finished there arose a great storm and brake it all to pieces. So soon as Xerxes heard what had befallen, he was very wroth, and commanded that they should lay three hundred lashes of the whip upon the Hellespont, and should also throw into the sea a pair of fetters. It has been said that he even sent branders to brand the Hellespont. Certainly he commanded them that laid the stripes on the water to say therewith barbarous and impious words: "O evil water, thy master putteth this punishment on thee because thou hast worked him harm that had worked no harm to thee. Know that King Xerxes will cross thee whether thou will or no. Rightly doth no man offer sacrifice to thee, deceitful and salt river as thou art." This punishment he bade them put upon the sea, and he cut off the heads of them that were set over the making of the bridge. Then they that had this thankless office put upon them fulfilled their task; and afterward other builders set about the work and accomplished it. They joined together ships of war, three hundred and sixty on the one side toward the Black Sea, and three hundred and fourteen on the other, mooring them with very great anchors that they might not be moved by the winds that blow either way. And they left three spaces that such as would pass by in light vessels, to or from the Black Sea, might do so without let. And when the bridge was finished, they made planks of wood of the same breadth as was the bridge, and laid them on the top; and on the planks they put brushwood, and on the brushwood earth; and when they had trodden this down they set up a barrier on either side, that the beasts of burden and the horses might not be afraid looking upon the sea.

But when the bridge had been finished, and the trench by Mount Athos, and the breakwater about the mouth of the trench—for they had made breakwaters by reason of the surf, that the mouth of the trench might not be filled up—it was now winter. Xerxes therefore passed the winter in Sardis; and when it was spring the army set forth.

On the very day of its setting forth the sun left its place in the heavens; and though there were no clouds, but the sky was at its clearest, the day was turned into night. When Xerxes saw this he was not a little troubled, and asked the Magians what this sight might mean. And the Magians made answer that the things signified to the Greeks the leaving of their cities; for that the sun was the foreteller to the Greeks and the moon to the Persians. But when Pythius the Lydian saw this marvel that had happened in the heavens, being emboldened by the gifts that he made to the King, he stood before Xerxes and said: "O my lord, I pray thee that thou grant me a certain thing which is of small account to thee, but to me very much to be desired." And Xerxes, not thinking what he had in his mind, made answer, "Speak on and I will do for thee whatsoever thou desirest." When Pythius heard these words he took courage and said, "O my lord, I have five sons, and thou art taking them all with thee for this war which thou makest against the Greeks. Have pity, therefore, on me, O King, remembering my old age, and release from this service one of my sons, even the eldest, that he may have me and my possessions in charge." When Xerxes heard this he was very wroth, and made answer, "Vile fellow, hast thou dared, even when I am myself going against Greece, and bringing with me my sons and my brethren, and my ministers and friends, to make mention of thy sons, thou that art my slave, and art bound to follow me with thy whole household, and even with thy wife. When thou didst well and madest to me offers of good things, thou couldst not surpass the King in bounty, and now that thou doest ill, thou shalt have less than thy desert. Thy hospitality shall save thee and four of thy sons; but the life of him whom thou lovest above the rest is the forfeit." So soon as Xerxes had said this, forthwith he gave command to them that had the charge of such things to search out the eldest of the sons of Pythius and cut him in twain; and when they had cut him in twain to put the two halves one on the right hand of the way and the other on the left. And he bade the army pass between the two. So the army passed between the two halves. First came they that bare the baggage, and the beasts of burden, and after them a great army of many nations, without any space between the nations, in all more than half of the whole. Then there was left a space between the host and the King. Afterward there came a thousand horsemen, chosen out of all the Persians, and after the horsemen a thousand spearmen, these too being chosen men, bearing their spear-points turned toward the ground, and after the spearmen ten horses of Nisa, having very fair trappings. These horses came from the plain of Nisa in the land of Media, and are very great. Behind the horses came the sacred chariot of Zeus, drawn by eight white horses, and after the horses there walked the charioteer on foot, holding the reins in his hand, for on the seat of this chariot no man may sit. After this came Xerxes himself, on a chariot drawn by horses of Nisa, and by his side was a charioteer, Patiramphes the son of Otanes. And whenever the wish took him he would change from his chariot to a litter. Behind the King came a thousand spearmen, the noblest and bravest of the Persians, holding their spears in the usual fashion; and after these a thousand chosen horsemen; and after the horsemen ten thousand chosen men on foot. A thousand of these had golden pomegranates instead of spikes at the shafts of their spears. These compassed about the other nine thousand, who had their spears with pomegranates of silver. The spearmen that pointed their spears to the ground had also pomegranates of gold, and those that came next after the King had apples of gold. After the ten thousand that were on foot came ten thousand horsemen of the Persians. Behind the horsemen was a space of two furlongs, after which came the remainder of the host, mingled in one crowd.

THE CHARIOT

As the host passed by Mount Ida there fell upon it a great storm of thunder and lightning, and slew many men. After this it came to the river Scamander; this was the first of the rivers that failed, being drunk up by the army and the horses and the beasts of burden. Here the King went up into the citadel of Priam, desiring to see the place; and when he had seen and heard every thing he sacrificed a thousand heifers to Athene of Troy; and the Magi poured out libations to the heroes. That night a panic fell upon the host; and so soon as it was day they departed and came to Abydos.

When he was come to Abydos Xerxes greatly desired to see his army. Now there had been prepared beforehand for him by the men of Abydos a seat of white marble on a hill that was nigh unto the city, for so he had bidden them. On this therefore he sat, and looking down upon the shore saw his army and his ships. And as he looked upon them he had a desire to see a race of ships; and there was made a race, and the Phœnicians of Sidon prevailed. Xerxes was greatly delighted with the contest and with the sight of his army. For when he saw all the Hellespont covered with ships, and all the shores and all the plains of Abydos filled with men, he counted himself a happy man. But afterward he wept.

And Artabanus, his uncle, the same that at the first spake boldly to the King that he should not make war against the Greeks, when he knew that Xerxes wept, went to him, and said, "O King, how different is this that thou doest now from that which thou didst but a short time ago? For then thou calledst thyself happy, but now thou weepest." Then said the King, "There came upon me of a sudden a thought of pity how short is the whole life of man, seeing that of all this great army not one shall be alive one hundred years hence." Then said Artabanus, "We men have to endure in life things more piteous than this. For in this life, for all its shortness, there is no man so happy but that he will wish, and this not once but many times, to die rather than to live. For misfortunes come upon us, and diseases harass us, so that life, though it be short, yet seems to be overlong, and death, so full of trouble is life, to be the best refuge to which a man can fly. For the Gods that give us a taste of the sweetness of life, yet are jealous so that we may not enjoy it to the full." To this Xerxes made answer, "Let us not so think of human life, though it be such as thou sayest, nor keep evil things in our minds when we have good things in our hands. But come now tell me, if thou hadst not seen that vision wouldst thou have been still of the same opinion, advising me that I should not make war against the Greeks." Artabanus answered, "O King, may the vision which we saw be accomplished as we would have it. Yet am I full of fear, seeing that there are two things, and these the greatest of all, that are against us." And the King said, "What are these two? Thinkest thou that the Greeks will bring against us more men or more ships?" Then said Artabanus, "No man that had any understanding could find any thing that he might blame either in thy host or thy fleet. Yet are two things against us, even the land and the sea. For there is, I suppose, no harbor in the sea so great that it could receive all this great multitude of ships; and yet we should have not one harbor, but many, one after the other, along the whole coast of the land. Seeing then that such harbors are not to be found, remember that chances are rulers of men rather than men of chances. And if the sea be hostile, much more is the land, and not the less so if none seek to withstand thee, seeing that the further thou shalt go the greater will be the danger of famine. This I say thinking it best for men to fear all things when they take counsel, and to fear nothing when they are in action."

Then said the King, "What thou sayest, Artabanus,

thou sayest not without reason. Yet if a man will always look to all chances that may happen he will never accomplish great deeds. Thou seest to what greatness this realm of Persia has grown. Yet if the kings that were before me had followed such councils as thine it had never grown in such fashion. Not without peril did they attain this glory, for great things are achieved by great dangers. We therefore follow in their steps, and having now set forth in the fairest season of the year, will return safe, when we have subdued all Europe; neither shall we meet with famine nor any evil thing whatsoever. For much food we carry with us, and we shall have the food of such nations as we shall subdue. And remember that it is against men that till the earth and not against wanderers that we go."

To this Artabanus made answer, "At the least, O King, hearken to one counsel which I would give thee. Cyrus the son of Cambyses subdued all the Ionians, save the Athenians only. I counsel thee, therefore, that thou do not by any means compel these Ionians to fight against their fathers. Surely without them we shall be stronger than our enemies. But if thou compel them, then must they either do a great wrong in fighting against the land that sent them forth, or do a righteous act going over from us to our enemies and thereby greatly injuring us."

To this Xerxes answered, "There is naught, Artabanus, in which thou hast gone further from the truth than in this judgment of thine concerning the Ionians. Have we not a sure proof of their truth—a thing of which both thou and all they that went with King

Darius against the Scythians are witnesses—that it was in their hands to destroy the army of the Persians or to save it alive. And they behaved themselves righteously, and did nothing unjust. And besides this, they have left their wives and children in our land. Why then should they think to rebel against us? But be of good heart; and go, take charge of my house and my kingdom. For to thee only of all the Persians do I commit my scepter."

So Xerxes sent Artabanus to Susa. And when he was departed he called together the noblest of the Persians, and said to them, "Men of Persia, I have called you together that I may bid you bear yourselves bravely, and do no shame to the deeds which the Persians in former days have wrought, for these have been great and worthy of renown. Do ye therefore one and all be zealous in this war, for we seek that which concerns us all. And, indeed, I am told that they are good men against whom we make war, and that if we conquer them there are none on the earth who can resist them. And now let us pray to the gods that have rule over Persia, and pass over the bridge."

So all that day they made preparations for the passing over; and the next day they waited for the rising of the sun, desiring to see it before they should begin to cross. And when the sun was risen, Xerxes, pouring drink offerings into the sea from a cup of gold, made his prayer with his face turned to the sun, that no misfortune might befall him before he should conquer all Europe, even to the uttermost borders. And when he had finished praying, he cast the cup into the Hellespont, and also a mixing bowl of gold, and a Persian sword which they call a cimeter. But whether he cast these things into the sea because he would offer them to the sun, or whether he repented him of having laid stripes upon the Hellespont and gave these gifts in atonement to the sea, can not certainly be known.

CHAPTER IX

HOW XERXES CROSSED OVER INTO EUROPE, AND OF HIS ARMY

ALL things being now ready, the host of Xerxes crossed over from Asia into Europe, the foot soldiers and the horsemen going over the bridge that was toward the Black Sea, and the servants of the army and the beasts of burden the bridge that was toward the Ægean. First came the Ten Thousand, all of them wearing crowns; and after them came a mixed host of all nations. These passed over on the first day; and on the next day passed over the horsemen, and they that carried their spears turned toward the ground. These also had crowns on their heads. After these came the sacred horses and the sacred chariot; and next to these Xerxes and the spearmen and the thousand horsemen, and after these the rest of the army. And all the ships sailed to the shore over against Abydos.

When Xerxes had crossed over, he watched his army crossing over under the lash, and this they did without pause or rest for seven days and seven nights. It is reported that when Xerxes had passed over a man that dwelt in these parts cried out, "O Zeus, why art thou come in the likeness of a Persian, and calling thyself Xerxes and not Zeus, with the whole race of men following thee, to destroy the Greeks, when thou couldst have destroyed them without so doing?"

When they had all crossed over there happened a great marvel, of which Xerxes took no account, though indeed it was easy to understand. The marvel was this, that a mare brought forth a hare. And what was to be understood from it was this—that Xerxes was leading against the Greeks a great host and splendidly equipped, and yet before many days he would come again to the same place as one that fled for life.

Then Xerxes went on his way, the fleet sailing along by the coast. And when he came to Doriscus he had a desire to know the number of his army. What indeed were the numbers of the several nations can not be said; but the number of the whole host was found to be a thousand thousand and seven hundred thousands. These were numbered in a way that shall now be told. They brought ten thousand men into one place; these they placed together as closely as they could, and having done this, they drew a circle about them; and when they had done this circle and let the ten thousand go, they made a heap about the circle, so high as the middle of a man. When they had so done they brought others into the place that was thus hedged about till they had filled it. When they had numbered the host they set it in order nation by nation.

These nations were many in number. First of all

were the Persians, wearing turbans on their heads and about their bodies tunics with sleeves of divers colors, having iron scales like to the scales of a fish. On their legs they had trews, and their shields were of wicker. For arms they had short spears and long bows and arrows of reed; also they had daggers hanging from their girdles by the right thigh. The Medes were accoutered in the same way; and indeed this fashion of armor is Median rather than Persian.

The Assyrians had helmets of brass, wrought in a strange fashion. These had shields and spears and daggers like to the Egyptians; and besides they had clubs of wood with knots of iron and linen corslets.

The Scythians had trews. These carried bows and daggers, and battle-axes also. The Indians were clad in cotton, with bows of cane, and arrows also of cane pointed with iron. As for the Arabians they had long cloaks bound about the waist with girdles, and at their right side they carried bows bending backward. They that came from Ethiopia were clad in skins of panthers and lions. Their bows were of the stems of palm leaves, four cubits and more in length; their arrows were small and of reed, having heads of stone for iron. (This same stone is used for engraving of seals.) They had spears also, with the horns of antelopes made sharp for spear-heads, and knotted clubs also. When they were about to go into battle they would paint the one half of their bodies with chalk and the other with vermilion. There were also Eastern Ethiopians (these had straight hair, while they of the West had hair more woolly than the hair of other men) equipped like to the others, but having the scalps of horses on their heads. These they flay off with the ears and mane. The ears stand upright and the mane is for a crest. For shields they have bucklers made of the skins of cranes.

Many nations came from the Lower Asia, as Phrygians and Paphlagonians, and Lydians, these last being clad and armed very much in Greek fashion. There were also Mysians (who in old time came forth from Lydia, but then dwelt in the Mysian Olympus). These had helmets and bucklers and staves of wood with one end hardened in the fire. Also the Bithynians came from this land, having before dwelt about the Strymon, in Thrace. These had skins of foxes on their heads, and tunics with long cloaks of many colors about their bodies, and buskins of fawn skins about their legs and feet; and for arms javelins and light shields and short daggers.

From these and many other nations of Asia and Africa came the footmen of the host. They had captains of tens and of hundreds and of thousands and of ten thousands; and over all six generals, Mardonius, Tritantæchmes, son of Artabanus, Megabyzus, son of Zopyrus, the same that took the city of Babylon for King Darius, and three others.

These six commanded all the footmen save only the Ten Thousand. These Ten Thousand were Persians all of them, chosen men. These Hydarnes led, and they were called the Immortals, because if any man among them die or fall sick, straightway another is chosen into his place, so that they are ten thousand always, neither more nor less. Of all the host the Persians were the bravest and most splendidly equipped.

The horsemen came from many nations. Among these were the Sagartians, a wandering people. These are wont to have no arms either of iron or bronze, save only a dirk. But they have lassoes of leathern thongs and trust to these. They fight in this fashion. When they go into battle, they cast their lassoes having nooses at the end; and that which is entangled in the noose they draw toward them, be it man or horse, and slay it.

Of the Indians some rode in chariots drawn by wild asses. The Arabians rode on camels that were not less swift than horses. These were set last in order because the horses could not endure the sight of the camels. Of horsemen there were in all eighty thousand.

The number of the ships of war was one thousand and two hundred and seven. Of these the Phœnicians furnished three hundred and the Egyptians two hundred, and the men of Cyprus one hundred and fifty, and the men of Cilicia one hundred. The Ionians and the Æolians and the Greeks that dwelt about the Hellespont and the Black Sea furnished two hundred and sixty and seven. And on all the ships there were fighting men, Persians and Medes and Sacæ. The best of all the ships were the Phœnician, and of the Phœnician ships the best they that came from Sidon.

As to the names of them that commanded the ships, there is no need to tell them. For indeed they were not commanders but slaves, even as the others. But the Persians that commanded were Ariabignes son of

Darius, and Megabazus, with two others. Of smaller ships and transports and the like there were three thousand in all.

One of the generals must needs be mentioned, namely Artemisia, the daughter of Lygdamis. She, her husband being dead and her son but a lad, had the lordship of her city, even Halicarnassus; and she went with Xerxes against Greece, not of necessity, but of her own free will, so valiant was she and of so manlike a spirit. She furnished five ships to the King, and in all the fleet there were none better, save only those of the Sidonians; nor was there one of the allies that gave better counsel to the King than did this Artemisia.

When Xerxes had numbered the host and the fleet, and had set them in order, it seemed good to him to go through them and see them for himself. This therefore he did. First he rode on a chariot, driving from nation to nation, and inquiring about each many things; and there followed scribes, who wrote down that which was answered. This he did till he came to the very end of the footmen and of the horsemen. After this he left his chariot and embarked on a ship of Sidon, and sitting under a tent of gold sailed along by the prows of the ships, these all having been launched and being drawn up about four hundred feet from the shore, and the fighting men upon them, some ready armed as for battle. The King sailed between the ships and the shore; and the scribes followed him and wrote as before.

When he had ended these things he sent for Demaratus, the son of Ariston, that had been King in Sparta, and had been banished thence, and asked him, saying, "Demaratus, it is my pleasure to ask thee a certain question. Thou art a Greek; and as I hear from thee and from other of thy people, thou comest of a city that is by no means the least or weakest in the land of Greece. Tell me, then, will the Greeks abide our coming, and lift a hand against us? For, as it seems to me, not all the Greeks, nor all the barbarians of the west, if they were gathered together, could stand up against me when I come against them, if they were not of one mind. But tell me, what thinkest thou?"

Then said Demaratus, "Shall I answer thee that which is true or that which is pleasant?"

The King said, "Speak that which is true. It shall not be the worse for thee."

When Demaratus heard this, he said, "O King, thou biddest me speak the truth, so that I may not be found hereafter to have lied unto thee. With us Greeks poverty is born and bred; and we have gotten for ourselves valor by help of wisdom and law, and by valor we keep ourselves both from poverty and from servitude. Now that which I am about to say regards the Spartans only, though indeed I honor all the Greeks that dwell in the Dorian country. Know then, in the first place, that the Spartans will receive no conditions from thee that shall bring slavery upon Greece; and in the second, that they will surely come forth to meet thee in battle, yea, though all the Greeks besides be on thy side. But as to their number there is no need to inquire; for if there be a thousand that shall march out to battle, or if there be more or less these will surely fight."

When Xerxes heard this he laughed, and said, "What is this that thou hast said, Demaratus? Shall a thousand men fight with a whole army? Tell me now. Thou hast been, thou sayest, King of these Spartans. Wilt thou then forthwith fight singly with ten men? Yet if all thy nation be such as thou sayest, thou being their King shouldst, according to your custom, contend against as many again; so that if a common man be a match for ten men of my army thou shouldst be a match for twenty. But if they that so boast themselves are no bigger or stronger than the Greeks that I have seen, thyself, to wit, and others, then is this talk but empty words. Consider now the likelihood of the thing. How could a thousand, or ten thousand, or even fifty thousand, stand up against such an army, the more so if they be free and not under the rule of one man? For say that there be five thousand of them, yet shall we have more than a thousand to one. If, indeed, they were under the rule of one man after our fashion, then might they for fear of him be valiant even beyond their nature, and fight few against many, being driven thereto by the lash. But being free, and left to choose, they will do neither the one nor the other. I verily believe that Greeks could scarce stand up in battle against Persians, the number being equal. But as to this, that one man can fight against many, we have indeed a few such in our army, but a few only, for some of my spearmen would not refuse to fight one man against three Greeks. But about this thou knowest nothing, and so talkest idly."

To this Demaratus made answer, "O King, I knew at the beginning that if I should speak the truth I should not please thee. But the truth thou wouldst have me speak; therefore I told thee the things that concerned the Spartans. And yet I love them not, as thou knowest very well, seeing that they took from me the place and dignity that came to me from my father, and drave me out into banishment, whereas thy father Darius received me and gave me sustenance and a home to dwell in; and it is not to be believed that a wise man would scorn such kindness, but rather that he would cherish it in his heart. For myself I engage not to fight with ten men, nor yet with two, nor indeed would I willingly fight with one; yet if there should be any necessity or great cause, I would gladly fight with any of the men who say they are a match for three Greeks. And as for the Spartans, when they fight singly they are as good as any men in the world; and when they fight together they are better than any. For though they be free, yet are they not wholly free. For they have a master over them, even Law, whom they fear more than thy people fear thee. Whatsoever this master commands, that they do. And he commands them that they turn not their backs in battle, how many soever be their enemies, but abide in their place, and conquer or die. If thou thinkest that these things that I say are naught, then will I hold my peace hereafter. Howbeit, I pray that all things may be as thou wouldst have them, O King."

This was the answer of Demaratus. And the King laughed, and sent him away in peace.

CHAPTER X

OF THE MARCH OF XERXES

XERXES made Mascames governor of the fort of Doricus. This man he esteemed very highly, sending him gifts every year; and Artaxerxes after him sent gifts to the children of Mascames. Nor, indeed was any of the Persian governors held in greater honor, save Boges only. This Boges was besieged in Eion that is on the river Strymon by Cimon and the Athenians. And though he might have made an agreement with them and come out from Eion and returned safe to Asia, he would not, lest he should seem to the King to have failed in valor, but held out to the last. And when there was no food remaining in the fort, he caused a great pile of wood to be built, and slew his children and his wife and his concubines and his slaves, and cast them into the fire. After this he threw all the gold and silver that was in the fort into the river; and last of all he cast himself into the fire. With good cause, therefore, do the Persians honor him to this day.

Then Xerxes went on his way from Doricus westward; and whomsoever he found he compelled to take service with him. The road by which he went the

Thracians in after time held in great honor, and did not plow it or sow it.

When the King came to Acanthus that is by Mount Athos, and saw what had been done with the trench, and knew that the people of Acanthus had been very zealous in the work, he sent them a Persian dress for a gift, and praised them much. While he tarried here Artachæes, a Persian, and of the royal house, who had been set over the digging of the trench, fell sick and died. He excelled in stature all the Persians, being but five fingers short of five cubits of the royal measure, and his voice surpassed that of other men. Wherefore the King was much troubled at his death, and buried him with great honor, and all the host made a mound over his grave. Afterward the people of Acanthus sacrificed to this man as to a hero, being bidden so to do by an oracle.

As for the Greeks that fed the army and entertained Xerxes, they were brought to great poverty, so that many of them were driven to forsake their homes. For when the people of Thasos, having possessions on the mainland, were commanded so to entertain the army of Xerxes, a certain Antipater, one of the chiefest of the citizens, having the charge of the matter, showed that there were expended on the meal four hundred talents of silver. In other cities also they that had this charge made the same reckoning. And, indeed, this entertainment was ordered many days beforehand, and was a matter of no small preparation. The manner of it was this. So soon as they received the commandment

OFFERINGS

from the heralds that were sent to give them warning, then the citizens set about grinding wheat and barley. This they did for many months. Also they fatted beasts, finding the best that they could buy; and they reared birds, both land-birds and water-birds, in buildings and ponds for the entertaining of the army. Also they prepared cups and bowls of gold and silver and all other things for the furniture of the table. This indeed they did for the King and for them that sat at meat with him only; but for the rest of the army they made ready only such food as had been commanded. For Xerxes a tent was made ready wherein he might lodge; but the rest of the army lodged without shelter. So soon as the time of eating came they that entertained had great toil and trouble; and the soldiers ate their fill and staid that night in the same place. The next day they tare down the tent and took all the furniture, leaving nothing, but carrying all away with them. Well therefore did Megacreon of Abdera speak when he counseled the men of Abdera to go with their wives and children to the temples, and after putting up prayers for the time to come, thank the Gods that it was not the pleasure of King Xerxes to have two meals in the day, for that verily if he had desired not only dinner but breakfast also, then must the people of Abdera have either fled from before the King or, awaiting his coming, have been utterly ruined.

At this town of Acanthus Xerxes commanded the fleet that it should sail through the trench by Mount Athos and should await his coming at Therma; but he himself led his army through the land of Pæonia. Here the camels that carried the victuals for the host were set upon by lions, which coming by night from their dens touched neither man nor beast but the camels only; but what it was that drave them to this, considering that they had never before seen the beast, or made any trial of it, no man can say. There are many lions in this country, and wild oxen also with very long horns, which are brought into Greece. So Xerxes came to Therma; and being at Therma he saw the two mountains Olympus and Ossa, which are indeed marvelously high. And when he heard that there was between these mountains a narrow pass through which ran a river, and that this was the road into Thessaly, he conceived a desire to go on shipboard and see the place where the river flowed into the sea. Wherefore he embarked on a ship of Sidon, the same that he was wont to use when he would go on such a journey, and gave the signal for the others to set sail also. And when he came to the place, he marveled much at the outflow of the rivers, and calling to him the guide would fain know whether it were possible to bring the rivers into the sea by any other way.

Men say that in old time Thessaly was a great lake, being shut in on every side by high mountains. And indeed toward the east Ossa and Pelion are joined together at the base, and on the north is Olympus, and on the west Pindus, and on the south Othrys. In this land there are many rivers which all make their way into the sea by one channel, even the Peneus. But they say that in old time this channel was not, but that afterward Poseidon made it; which may well be if Poseidon brings earthquakes to pass, and if chasms are his handiwork. For it is manifest that the hills have been torn asunder by an earthquake. When therefore Xerxes asked the guides whether the water could pass by any other outlet into the sea, the men, as knowing the nature of the place, made answer, "There is no other way, O King, by which this water can pass into the sea save this which thou now seest; for Thessaly is girded about with hills."

Then said Xerxes, "The men of Thessaly are wise. Good reason had they to change their minds in time and to make provision for their safety. For, not to speak of other things, they knew that they dwelt in a land which it was easy to subdue. For nothing was needed save to turn the river upon their lands, building up a mound in this channel, and so turning the stream from its course. So would all Thessaly be changed into a lake."

When the King said this he thought of the sons of Aleuas, who had made their submission to him first of all the Greeks, being Thessalians. And he thought that they had done this in the name of the whole people. After this the King went back to Therma. And here there came to him the heralds whom he had sent to the Greek cities demanding earth and water, some being empty-handed and some carrying that for which they had been sent. Many nations gave earth and water, as the Thessalians and the Locrians and the Bœotians; only the men of Platæa and Thespiæ, that are towns of the Bœotians, gave them not. Against all such the Greeks that stood up against the barbarians sware this oath: "From all people who being Greeks have given themselves up to the Persians, without necessity compelling, we will take a tithe of their goods, and offer it to the god at Delphi."

Now it must be remembered that Xerxes, though he said that he was marching against Athens, had it in his mind to subdue all Greece. And this the Greeks knew beforehand, though indeed they did not all regard the matter in the same way. For some had no fear of the barbarians, as having given them earth and water, and thinking therefore that they should receive from them no harm; but others, having not given these things, were in great fear. For whereas they thought that all the ships in Greece were not enough to meet the Persians, so also they knew that the greater part of the cities would take no part in the war, but greatly favored the enemy.

And here must be said a thing which because it is

true ought to be said, though most men will mislike it. If the Athenians, for fear of the danger that was coming upon them, had left their country, or, not leaving it, had submitted themselves to Xerxes, then certainly none would have sought to withstand the Persians by sea; and if none had withstood the Persians by sea, then there would have come to pass on the land what shall now be set forth. Though many breastworks had been built across the Isthmus, yet would the Lacedæmonians have been betrayed by their allies; not of their free will, indeed, but because their cities would have been taken, one after the other, by the fleet of the barbarians. So would they in the end have been left alone, and being so left alone, after many deeds of valor, would have perished with great glory. Or if not, then seeing beforehand that all the other Greeks were submitting themselves to the Persians, they also would have made an agreement with Xerxes. So, in either case, would Greece have been made subject to the barbarians. For what would have been the profit of walls built across the Isthmus while the King had the mastery by sea? If a man then should say that in truth the Athenians were the saviours of Greece, he would speak truly; for to whichever side they had inclined that would have been the weightier. And they, having a fixed purpose that Greece should be free, stirred up all the nations that had not submitted themselves to the Persians, and so, next to the Gods, drave back the enemy.

And this they did though they were sorely terrified by the oracle. For when they sent messengers to inquire of the god at Delphi, and these had offered sacrifices after the custom, and were now come into the shrine, the priestess gave to them this answer. (The name of the priestess was Aristonice).

> "Why sit ye still? Fly, wretched race,
> To earth's far bounds the fatal place.
> Fly hearth and home and craggy hill,
>   Round which the wheel-like city stands;
> Through all her being fares she ill,
>   Body, and head, and feet, and hands.
> The fire consumes them, and from far,
> Wild Ares drives his Syrian car.
> Full many a tower, both fair and tall,
> Not thine alone, before him fall;
> Full many a holy place and shrine
>   The fire's devouring flames shall seize;
> Cold stands the sweat on face divine,
>   And shake with fear the trembling knees;
> From high-pitched roof the blood-drops fall,
>   Fell signs of storm and coming woe;
> Leave, suppliant band, Apollo's hall,
> Prepare you for the fate ye know."

When the messengers from Athens heard these words they were greatly troubled. But Timon the son of Androbulus, a chief man among the citizens of Delphi, seeing how utterly cast down they were by the evil that was prophesied concerning their country, counseled them that they should take tokens of suppliants in their hands, and in this guise go and inquire of the oracle once more. This then the Athenians did, and spake, saying, "O King, prophesy unto us some better thing about our country, having regard to these tokens of suppliants which we bring into thy presence. Else will we not depart from thy sanctuary, but will abide here till the day of our death." Then the priestess prophesied to them a second time, using these words:

"Pallas desires with deep desire
To change the purpose of her sire.
Again entreats him, and again;
But vain her prayers, her counsel vain.
Yet sons of Athens, hear once more
  The firm, unyielding word of fate;
  Whene'er the fair Cecropian state,
From bound to bound and shore to shore
Before the foeman's might shall bow,
One boon will Zeus All-wise allow
To Pallas' prayer—that ne'er shall fall
Fair Athens' stay, her wooden wall:
Think not to wait that evil hour
Horsemen or footmen's dark array;
Fly, fly their host; yet comes the hour
Ye stand to meet the foemen's power.
Thou, holy Salamis, shalt bring
  Dark death to sons of women born,
Or when abroad the seed they fling,
  Or when they pluck the ripened corn."

These words seemed to be, as indeed they were, milder than the former words. So the envoys wrote them down, and returned with them to Athens.

CHAPTER XI

OF THE PREPARATIONS
OF THE GREEKS

WHEN the messengers told the words that they had heard and written down to the people, there were many and various opinions among those who sought to interpret the oracle. Some of the older men said that it seemed to them that the god bade them fortify the citadel, for that in old time the citadel of Athens had been surrounded with a fence. And this fence they supposed to be the "wooden wall." And there were others that said the "wooden wall" signified their ships; but these were confounded by the last words of the oracle:

> "Thou, holy Salamis, shalt bring
> Dark death to sons of women born,
> Or when abroad the seed they fling,
> Or when they pluck the ripened corn."

These words troubled them much, for the readers of oracles declared that it was signified by them that they should fight in ships and be worsted at Salamis.

Now there was at Athens a certain man that was

but newly risen into the front rank of the citizens. This was Themistocles the son of Neocles. He then coming forward affirmed that the oracle-readers did not read the words aright, for that, if they had been really spoken concerning the Athenians, the god would have said, "Sad Salamis," rather than "Holy Salamis," it being decreed that the dwellers in the land should die there. It was manifest therefore, he said, to one that interpreted the words aright that they were spoken concerning the barbarians, and not concerning the Athenians. Wherefore he advised his fellow-citizens that they should make ready to fight in ships, for that these were their "wooden wall." When Themistocles had set forth these opinions, the Athenians judged them to be better than the opinions of the oracle-readers. For these would have hindered them from fighting in ships, yea, from so much as lifting up their hands against the enemy, and would have had them leave their country, and find some other wherein to dwell.

Before this, another counsel of this same Themistocles had been given excellently in season. It so chanced that the Athenians had much money in their public treasury, having received it from their mines at Laurium. This they were about to divide among the citizens, man by man, so that each should have ten drachmæ; but Themistocles persuaded the Athenians that this division should not be made, but that they should use the money for the building of two hundred ships for the war that they had on hand, that is to say, the war against Ægina. This war indeed it was that was the saving of Greece, for it compelled the Athenians to become seafaring men. As for the two hundred ships, they were not used for the end for the which they were made; but they were a help to Greece when she most needed them. So many ships had the Athenians ready before the war; and they began to build others. And now, after hearing the oracle and consulting thereupon, they judged it well to put their whole force on shipboard, even as the god commanded them; and so, together with such of the Greeks as were of the same mind, to give battle to the barbarians.

So soon as the Greeks that followed the good cause, even the cause of Greece, were assembled together, they took counsel and pledged their faith one to the other. This being done, they agreed in this, that, first of all, all feuds that there were of nation against nation should be appeased. Many such there were; but the greatest of all was that between the men of Athens and the men of Ægina. Afterward, when they knew that King Xerxes had come down to Sardis with his host, they thought it good to send spies to see how matters stood with the King in Asia; also they sent embassadors, some to Argos, to make an alliance against the Persians; and others to Sicily, to Gelon, lord of Syracuse; and to Corcyra, to ask for help; and others again to Crete. For they desired to bind together into one all that bare the Greek name, so that they might strive with one heart against him that was the enemy of all. Now the power of Syracuse was said to be greater than the power of any other city among the Greeks.

When they had thus taken counsel together, and had caused all such as were at enmity to be reconciled, they sent three men into Asia to be spies. These came to Sardis and learned what was to be known about the King's army. But being discovered, they were questioned by the generals and condemned to die. But when Xerxes heard this he blamed the purpose of the generals, and sent some of his own spearmen, commanding that if they found the spies yet alive they should bring them into his presence. So the spearmen went, and finding them yet alive brought them into the presence of the King. And when the King saw them, he inquired of them wherefore they had come; and afterward commanded the spearmen that they should show them the whole army, both horse and foot, and all the power of the King, and that when the men had had their fill of this sight, they should send them away unhurt whithersoever they would. And the cause, he said, why he gave this commandment about the spies was this. If these spies be put to death, the Greeks will not know that my power is greater by far than all that they have heard, nor shall we harm them much slaying three of their men. But if these spies return to Greece, then will the Greeks hear the truth about this my host, and of their own free will they will give themselves to us and surrender their freedom, and we shall be spared the trouble of this great business. At another time, also, Xerxes spake much in the same fashion. When he was in Abydos he saw three corn ships coming from the Black Sea and sailing down the Hellespont, carrying wheat to Ægina and the Peloponnesus. And they that sat by him when they knew that the ships belonged to the enemy had thought of taking them, and looked to the King that he should give the word. Then said Xerxes, "Whither do these ships sail?" And the men answered, "To thy enemies, O King, carrying corn to them." Then the King said, "And are we not also sailing to the same place, taking with us corn as well as many other things? What wrong therefore do these men carrying food for us?" So it came to pass that the spies returned safe to Greece.

After this the Greeks sent messengers to divers cities, asking help. First they sent them to Argos. Now the Argives had been warned by an oracle that they should sit quiet, being indeed greatly weakened by that which they had suffered at the hands of the Spartans, for these, under King Cleomenes, had slain six thousand citizens. Nevertheless they bade the messengers come into their council chamber and declare their message. And when they had heard it they answered, "We will help you if the Spartans will give us a truce for thirty years, and will also divide with us the command of the army. This indeed we should by rights have altogether, but we will divide it with Sparta. The truce they asked that, their children having grown to man's estate, they might be able to make head against Sparta, if need should be. The Spartans answered, "As for the truce, we will bring the matter before the people, but the leadership we can not divide as ye would have it. For we have two kings and ye only one. But your King shall have one vote." This the Argives could not endure. Whereupon they said to the messengers, "Depart out of our borders before the sun be set, or we will deal with you as with enemies."

This is the story of the Argives, but the other Greeks affirm that Xerxes sent a messenger to them, saying,

"We Persians are your kinsmen, for Perses, who is our father, was son to Perseus that was the son of Danae, that was the daughter of Acrisius your King. Wherefore neither should we fight against you, nor ye against us. Do ye, therefore, keep quiet, and there shall be none whom we will honor more than you." With this message the Argives were greatly pleased; and they asked for a share in the leadership for a pretense only, as knowing that the Spartans would not yield it.

Many years after it chanced that while certain ambassadors from Athens were at Susa, there came up also an embassy from Argos, who inquired of King Artaxerxes, that was son to Xerxes, "Does the friendship that Xerxes thy father made with us still remain, or dost thou count us as enemies?" To this Artaxerxes answered that the friendship remained, and that he held no city dearer to him than Argos.

The truth of these matters can not certainly be known. Yet so much may be affirmed without doubt, that if all men were to bring their own misdeeds into one place, as wishing to exchange them for the misdeeds of their neighbors, when they came to look close into the misdeeds of their neighbors, they would be right glad to carry back their own.

Other messengers, among whom was one Syagrus of Sparta, were sent to speak with Gelon, lord of Syracuse. These, when they were come into his presence, spake, saying, "The Spartans and the Athenians and their allies have sent us to tell thee that the Persians are marching into Europe, giving out indeed that they make war upon Athens only, but purposing to subdue the whole land of Greece. Do thou therefore—for thou hast great power, being lord of Sicily—help us that we may keep our freedom. And be sure that if thou suffer us to perish these barbarians will fall next upon thee, and that if thou helpest us thou helpest thyself." To this Gelon made answer, "Men of Greece, ye think only of yourselves when ye ask my help against the Persians. Did ye help me when I would have had you for my allies against the Carthaginians? Nevertheless I will not render evil for evil, but will help you, sending two hundred ships, and twenty thousand footmen, and two thousand horsemen, and archers and slingers and light horsemen, of each two thousand. Also I will promise meat for the whole host of the forces so long as the war shall continue. Only ye must make me commander."

Therefore Syagrus the Spartan burst forth, "Surely now Agamemnon son of Pelops would groan to hear that Gelon and the men of Syracuse had taken the leadership from Sparta. If thou wilt help the Greeks, O King, know that thou must follow the leading of the Spartans."

Then said Gelon, "For all thy evil words, man of Sparta, thou shalt not persuade me to answer thee evil. Yet if ye put such store by this command, how much more should I, that can bring with me so great an army! Howbeit I will yield to you so much as this. If ye will take the rule of the army, then will I command the ships; or, if ye choose the ships, yield the army to me. But if this please you not, then ye must depart without my alliance."

Then said the ambassador from Athens, making haste before the Spartan could speak, "The Greeks have sent me, O King, to ask not for a leader, but for an army; but thou sayest little of an army, but art over eager for the leadership. As to the army we were willing that the Spartan should answer; but as to the fleet, hear this. If the Spartans will have the command, we yield it to them; but if not, then it comes to us, and we give it to no man. For why should we yield, who are the most ancient nation of all the Greeks, and of whom came the most skillful to order an army of all the chieftains that fought against Troy?"

Then said Gelon, "Man of Athens, ye seem to have commanders more than enough, but of them that should be commanded a few only. Go ye back then to Greece with all haste, and say that she has lost the spring out of the year." For he likened himself and his power to the spring, which is the best season of the year.

When the Greeks had departed, Gelon sent three small ships, and with them one Cadmus, who should watch the issue of the war. And the man had with him many gifts and earth and water. These Gelon commanded him to give to King Xerxes if he should get the upper hand, and if not, to bring back again. This Cadmus had received the lordship of Cos from his father, yet for love of right and justice gave it up to the people. And in this manner also he showed himself to be a righteous man; for when the Greeks had prevailed, and Xerxes had departed, he kept not the gifts, as he might have done, but carried them back to Gelon.

Nevertheless some say that, notwithstanding the matter of the leadership, Gelon would have helped the Greeks, but that there came to Sicily about this time a great army of Phœnicians and Libyans and Sardinians under Hamilcar, King of Carthage. They say also that he conquered this army on the very same day on which the Greeks conquered the Persians at Salamis.

Envoys went also to the Corcyreans, who spake them fair, saying that they would send sixty ships. But these ships were long delayed; and after they had set forth they lingered about the coast of the Peloponnese, waiting for the end, even as did Gelon. But when the Greeks reproached them, the Corcyreans answered that the Etesian winds had not suffered them to round Cape Malea.

The Cretans inquired of the god of Delphi whether they should help the Greeks; and the god answered them, "Do ye not remember, ye fools, how that Minos was wroth with your nation because ye went to help the Greeks against Troy, because forsooth a barbarian had carried off a woman from Sparta, yet cared not to avenge him when he perished at Camicus?" Wherefore the men of Crete sat still.

While these things were being done the men of Thessaly sent to the Greeks, saying, "Come ye and guard the pass of Olympus, so shall ye preserve both our country and the rest of Greece also. But if ye will not, then must we yield to the Persians, lest we be left alone and so perish on your behalf."

Then the Greeks sent an army, even ten thousand

men at arms, to the Pass of Olympus. But when they had been there a few days only there came messengers from Alexander, King of Macedon, saying, "Depart from this place lest ye be trampled underfoot by your enemies." And he told them of the number of the army and of the ships. So the Greeks departed and returned to the Isthmus; and having taken counsel again, they determined to send an army to Thermopylæ, which is the Pass from Thessaly into Greece. And the fleet they sent to Artemisium, which is in the island of Eubœa. As for the Pass it is but fifty feet wide, and westward there is a high mountain which no man can climb, but to the eastward is the sea and the marshes of the river Peneus. And across this Pass there had been built a wall in old time. The Phocians built it for fear of the men of Thessaly. And now the Greeks repaired the breaches, for it was broken down.

In the meanwhile the men of Delphi inquired of the god what they should do, being in great fear of the barbarians. And the god said to them that they should pray to the winds. To the Athenians also there came an oracle that they should seek help from their son-in-law. Now their son-in-law was Boreas, the north-wind; for Boreas, being a prince of Thrace, took to wife, as say the Greeks, Orithyia, the daughter of Erechtheus, that was King of Athens.

CHAPTER XII

OF THE ARMY AND THE SHIPS OF XERXES, AND OF THE FIRST FIGHTING WITH THE GREEKS

KING Xerxes brought with him from Asia twelve hundred and seven great ships; and in each ship there were two hundred rowers and thirty fighting men. Also he had of smaller ships, having fifty oars or under, three thousand, and in each of these, taking one with another, there were eighty men. Therefore the whole number of the men that served on the ships was five hundred and seventeen thousand and six hundred. Of foot soldiers there were seventeen hundred thousand, and of horsemen eighty thousand, and of Arabs riding on camels and of Libyans that fought from chariots twenty thousand. There were also one hundred and twenty ships of Greeks that dwelt in Thrace and in the islands thereof, and in these twenty and four thousand men. To these must be added foot soldiers of the Thracians, the Pæonians, the Macedonians, and others. And the sum of the whole was two million six hundred and forty-one thousand six hundred and ten. And of all this great host there was none fitter to be the ruler for beauty and great stature than King Xerxes himself. Of those that followed the camp, and of the crews of the provision ships and other vessels of transport, the number was more rather than less the number of the fighting men. As for the women that ground the corn, and others that came with the army, and the horses, and the beasts of burden, and the dogs, their number can not be told.

The fleet, departing from Therma, came to the country of Magnesia and there cast anchor. But ten of the swiftest ships sailed down the gulf of Therma straight to the island of Sciathos, which lies to the northward of Eubœa. Here were three ships of the Greeks, whereof one was from Athens, and one from Ægina, and one from Trœzen; these were looking out for the coming of the barbarians. And when they spied the ships of the barbarians they fled with all speed, and the barbarians pursued them, and overtook the ship of Trœzen. Then they took the most beautiful of the fighting men and sacrificed him at the prow of the ship, thinking that this was an omen of good to them, for the man was very beautiful, and was the first captive they had taken from the Greeks. Also his name was Leo, that is to say, Lion; and this was another cause for which they sacrificed him.

The ship of Ægina gave the Persians no small trouble, a certain Pytheas, who was a fighting man thereon, bearing himself very bravely. For when the ship was taken he did not cease to contend with the enemies, until he fell, being covered with wounds from head to foot. But the Persian soldiers, finding that he was not dead, but still breathed, made much of him, seeking to keep him alive. His wounds they dressed with myrrh and bound with bandages of cotton; and when they came back to their encampment they showed the man to the host, admiring him and dealing with him kindly. But with the rest of the crew they dealt as with slaves.

As for the Athenian ship, it was run aground at the mouth of the river Peneus. The men leaped ashore and escaped through Thessaly, but the ship was taken by the barbarians. When the rest of the Greeks knew of the coming of the barbarians they were sore afraid, and departed from Artemisium, intending to defend the Euripus. Now the Euripus lies to the southward, where the strait between the island of Eubœa and the mainland is the narrowest.

And now there befell the first disaster that came upon the Persians. When the fleet cast anchor on the coast of Magnesia, the first row of ships was anchored to the shore, and the next row was without these, and the whole number of the rows was eight, one after the other for the beach was very small. The night indeed was calm; but at dawn there fell upon them a strong wind from the east, which the dwellers in these parts call the wind of the Hellespont. Such as knew the storm coming, and were able to drag their ships on to the shore, saved themselves, but of the others many were broken to pieces. Thus it was, say the Athenians, that Boreas, their son-in-law, helped them and when they returned to their country they built a temple to him on the banks of the river Ilissus. Of the Persian ships there were broken, at the least, four hundred. There were drowned also men without number, and much treasure was lost. Of this treasure, indeed, one Ameinocles, a Magnesian, made much gain, gathering gold and silver cups which were washed up by the sea, and treasure boxes of the Persians, and articles of gold without number. Thus he became very rich, but had trouble withal, losing his children by violence.

For three days the storm endured. But the Magians offering victims and using incantations and doing sacrifices to Thetis and the nymphs of the sea, laid it on the fourth day, or, may be, it ceased of its own accord. The cause wherefore they offered sacrifices to Thetis was that here Peleus carried her off to be his wife.

When the Greeks heard from their watchers—for they had all watchers on the hills of Eubœa—of the storms and of the breaking of the Persian ships, they hastened back with all speed to Artemisium, thinking to find a few ships only to fight with. And ever after they were wont to speak of Poseidon as the Preserver.

When the storm had ceased, the barbarians sailed to Aphetæ, that is a harbor on the mainland over against Artemisium. But fifteen ships having lagged behind, fell into the hands of the Greeks, for they took the Greek ships for their own, and sailed into the midst of them: a certain Sandoces was commander of the fifteen. This man had been governor of Cumæ in Æolia, and being one of the royal judges had been crucified by King Darius because he had taken a bribe. But while he hung upon the cross, the King found that the good deeds which he had done to the King's house were more than his evil deeds, and commanded that he should be taken down. Thus he escaped with his life; but this second peril he did not escape.

THE HORSE RACE

In the meanwhile Xerxes with the host passed through the land of Thessaly. Here he matched his horses with the horses of Thessaly, hearing that these were the swiftest in all Greece; and the horses of Thessaly were far outstripped. And having passed through Thessaly he came to Trachis.

CHAPTER XIII

OF THE BATTLE OF THERMOPYLÆ

KING XERXES pitched his camp in the region of Trachis, and the Greeks pitched their camp in the Pass. (This Pass is called Thermopylæ, that is to say, the Hot Gates, by the greater part of the Greeks, but the inhabitants of the country call it Pylæ, that is to say, the Gates.) Here then the two armies were set over against each other, the one being master of all the country from the Pass northward, and the other having that which lay to the southward. Now the Greeks that abode the coming of the Persians in this place were these—three hundred Spartans, heavy-armed men; and men of Tegea and Matinea a thousand, from each five hundred, and from Orchomenus one hundred and twenty, and from the rest of Arcadia a thousand. From Corinth there came four hundred, and from Phlius two hundred, and from Mycenæ eighty. So many came from the Peloponnesus; of the Bœotians there came seven hundred from Thespiæ and four hundred from Thebes. Besides these there had come at the summons the Locrians of Opus with all the men that they had, and a thousand Phocians. For these the other Greeks had summoned to their help, saying to them by messengers, "We all that are here are come but as the vanguard of the host; as for the others we look for their coming day by day. The sea also is in safe keeping, being watched by the men of Athens and the men of Ægina, and such others as have been appointed to this work. Remember also that he who now comes against Greece is no god, but a man only; nor is there any mortal, nor ever will be, with whom from the very day of his birth misfortune is not always close at hand, and the greater the man the greater also the misfortune. Wherefore it may be believed that he who now comes against us, being but a mortal man, may fail of his purpose." When the Phocians and Locrians heard these words, they came to the help of the Greeks at Trachis. All of these had commanders of their own, for every city one; but he that was most admired and had the chief command of the army was a Spartan, Leonidas by name, being the twenty-first in descent from Hercules, and having obtained the kingdom in Sparta contrary to expectation. For he had two brothers that were older than he, to wit, Cleomenes and Dorieus, and so had no thoughts of the kingdom. Nevertheless, when Cleomenes died without male offspring, and Dorieus also was dead, having perished in Sicily, the kingdom came to Leonidas, for he was older than Cleombrotus. (This Cleombrotus was the youngest of the sons of Anaxandrides.) This Leonidas had to wife Gorgo the daughter of Cleomenes; and now he went to Thermopylæ, taking with him three hundred men according to the custom of the kings of Sparta. These three hundred he had chosen from such

as had male children. On his way he took with him
the four hundred men of Thebes, their commander
being Leontiades. Now the cause why Leonidas made
much account of taking these men rather than any other
of the Greeks was this. It was commonly laid to the
charge of the Thebans that they favored the cause of the
Persians. For this cause he summoned them to the war,
seeking to know whether they would send the men or
would plainly refuse the alliance of the Greeks. And the
Thebans, though they wished otherwise, nevertheless
sent the men. The Spartans indeed sent on Leonidas
and his company beforehand, purposing themselves to
follow. For they thought that when the allies knew that
these were already gone, they would also make ready;
and they feared lest these should favor the Persians,
if they themselves should be seen to linger. And they
purposed, when they should have kept the feast—for
it chanced to be the feast of the Carneia—to leave a
garrison in Sparta, and to follow with their whole
force. And the rest of the allies were minded to do the
same thing; and it so befell that the festival of Olympia
was being kept at this time. But when they sent these
men before them, they had no thought that matters at
Thermopylæ would be brought to an end so speedily.

Now the Greeks that were at Thermopylæ, when
they saw that the Persians were now near to the mouth
of the Pass, were sore afraid, and took counsel together
whether they should not depart. The Peloponnesians,
for the most part, desired to return to the Peloponnesus
and guard the Isthmus; but Leonidas, seeing that the
Phocians and Locrians were greatly vexed at this counsel,

gave his sentence that they should remain, and should send messengers to the cities of the Greeks, bidding them send all the help that they could, for that they were over few to stand up against so great a host.

While the Greeks were holding a council on this matter, Xerxes sent a scout, a horseman, to see how many in number they were, and what they were doing. Now the man heard, while he was yet in Thessaly, that a small company of men were gathered together in this place, the chief of them being Spartans, and the leader King Leonidas, of the house and lineage of Hercules. And when he rode up to the place where the army was encamped, he saw a part of the men. The whole army he saw not, for they had built again the wall that was across the Pass, and were guarding it; and they that were within the wall he saw not; but they that were without the wall, having their arms piled beside them, he saw. Now it so chanced that they who had their place at the time without the wall were the Spartans. These the horseman saw busy with exercises and combing their hair. All this he much marveled to see, finding also how few they were in number. And when he had learned every thing for certain, he rode back again in peace; for no one pursued after him, or indeed paid him any heed whatsoever. And when he was come back he told Xerxes all the things that he had seen. But when Xerxes heard these things he could by no means understand that which was indeed the truth; how these men were making ready to slay as many as might be of their enemy, and so perish. Thinking therefore that the whole thing was but foolishness, he sent for Demaratus, for the man was yet with the army. And when Demaratus stood before him he asked him about these things, desiring to know what they signified. And Demaratus said, "Thou hast heard from me, O King, the truth concerning these men before this, even when we were first beginning this war; but when thou heardest it thou didst but laugh at me, though I told thee that which I knew would surely come to pass. For indeed, O King, I strive always with my whole heart to tell thee the truth. Hear, therefore, yet again what I say. These men are come hither to contend with us for the Pass; and this they now prepare to do; and they have this custom among them, that when they are about to put their lives in peril they adorn their heads with exceeding care. Know, also, O King, that if thou canst subdue these men, and such others of their nation as have been left behind in Sparta, there is no nation upon the earth that will abide thy coming or lift up a hand against thee; for this city that thou now fightest against is the most honorable in all Greece, and these men are the bravest."

But these things seemed to Xerxes to be wholly beyond belief; and he asked again the second time, "In what manner will these men, being so few, as we know them to be, fight with my great army?"

But Demaratus answered this only, "O King, deal with me as with a liar if every thing fall not out even as I have said." Notwithstanding, he could not persuade the King that it was so in truth.

Four days, therefore, did the King suffer to pass, hoping always that the Greeks would flee away from their place. But on the fifth day, seeing that they were not departed, but were full, as it seemed to him, of impudence and folly, he grew angry, and sent against them the Medes and the Cissians, giving them a command that they should take these Greeks alive and bring them before him. But when these men came up and fell upon the Greeks, many of them were slain. Then others came up into their places and ceased not from fighting, though indeed they suffered a very grievous slaughter, so that it was manifest to all men, and more especially to the King, that though he had very many that bore arms, yet had he but few men of war. And this battle endured throughout the whole day.

The Medes, having been thus roughly handled, fell back, and the Persians took up the fighting in their place, even the Ten Thousand, that had the name of the Immortals, whom Hydarnes commanded. These men thought to finish the matter very speedily. Nevertheless, when they came to deal with the Greeks, they accomplished nothing more than had the Medes, but fared just as ill, for indeed they fought in a narrow place, and their spears were shorter than the spears of the Greeks, and their numbers availed them not at all. As for the Spartans they fought in a notable way, showing themselves more skillful by far in battle than were their enemies. Then they would sometimes turn their backs, and make as though they were all fled; and when the barbarians saw them flee they would pursue after them with much shouting and uproar. Then the Spartans would turn again and stand face to face with the barbarians; and when they turned they would slay such multitudes as could not be counted. Here also there fell certain of the Spartans, but a few only. In the end, when the Persians after many trials could not by any means gain the Pass, neither by attacking in division nor by any other means, they went back to their camp. And twice, while these battles were being fought, did Xerxes leap from his seat in great fear for his army.

The next day also the barbarians fought, but fared no better than before; for they hoped that the Greeks, being few in number, had been overcome with their wounds, and would not be able any more to stand up against them. But these had been ordered in companies, according to their nations, and so fought, the one coming in the place of another. Only the Phocians did not fight, being set over the mountain that they might guard the path. Wherefore the Persians, finding that they prevailed not one whit more than before, turned back to the camp.

The King, therefore, was greatly perplexed what he should do. But while he considered there came to him a certain Ephialtes, a man of Malea, and desired to talk with him. This man, hoping to receive a great reward from the King, discovered to him the path that led over the mountain to Thermopylæ. Thus did he bring to destruction the Greeks that abode in the Pass. In after time, for fear of the Spartans, this man fled into Thessaly. And when he fled the wardens of the Pass put a price upon his life. This they did when the Amphictyons met at Pylæ. And as time went on Ephialtes came back from banishment and went to Anticyra. There a certain

Athenades slew him, not for this treachery, but for some other cause. But the Spartans honored Athenades not the less on this account. This was the end of Ephialtes. As for the other story, that there were two others, to wit, Phanagoras and Corydallus, that led the Persians by this path, it is not to be believed. For the wardens of the Pass set a price not on these two but on Ephialtes, having without doubt a perfect knowledge of the whole matter. Also it is well known that Ephialtes went into banishment for this cause. Let him therefore be named as having done this great wickedness.

The King was greatly pleased at the thing which this man undertook, that is to say, the showing of the path; and he sent Hydarnes and the Ten Thousand that were called the Immortals. These setting out from the camp about the time of the lighting of the lamps, crossed over the river Asopus, and marched all night, having Œta on their right and Trachis on their left. And when it was morning they were found close to the top of the mountain. At the first, indeed, the Phocians that had been set to guard the path knew not of their coming for the whole of the mountain was covered with a wood of oak trees. But when they came near, the morning being calm, there was heard a loud rustling, as indeed could not but be, the Persians treading the leaves under their feet. Then the Phocians leaped up and took their arms, and forthwith the barbarians appeared; and the Phocians, when they saw the armed men, were greatly astonished; for when they had not thought to deal with any enemy whatsoever, lo! there was an army at hand. Hydarnes indeed was much troubled, fearing that the men that he saw were Spartans. And he enquired of Ephialtes who they might be; and when he knew the certainty of the matter he commanded the Persians to make them ready for battle. Then the Phocians, finding that the arrows fell very thickly upon them, and thinking that the Persians were set upon their destruction, fled to the top of the mountain, and prepared to meet their death. But Hydarnes and Ephialtes took no heed of them, and went down the side of the mountain with all the speed they could.

As for the Greeks that were in the Pass, they knew of the doom that should come upon them so soon as the day appeared, first of all from the soothsayer Megistias (for Megistias learned it from the sacrifices). Afterward came in certain deserters with tidings that the Persians had made a compass by the path across the mountains; lastly, when the day was breaking, came the scouts running down from the hills. Then the Greeks held a council, considering what they should do; and they were divided; for some would not leave the post where they had been set, and others were very eager to depart. And when the council was broken up, some departed going each to their own cities, and others made ready to abide in the Pass with Leonidas. Some say indeed that Leonidas sent away them that departed, having a care for their safety; but it did not become him and the Spartans that were with him, he said, to leave their post that they had come to keep at the first. And indeed it seems fit to be believed that Leonidas, seeing that the others were fainthearted and would not willingly abide the peril, bade them go, but that he himself held it to be a shameful thing to depart. For he knew that he should get for himself great glory by abiding at his post, and that the prosperity of Sparta should not be destroyed. For when the Spartans at the very beginning of the war sent to inquire of the Pythia, seeking to know what should befall them, there was given to them an oracle, that one of two things must come to pass, to wit, that Sparta must perish, or that one of their kings must fall in battle.

And that oracle was this—

> "Dwellers in Sparta's proud domains,
> Hear what the will of fate ordains:
> Or falls your noble city low
> Beneath the feet of Persian foe;
> Or all your borders shall bewail
> A Zeus-descended monarch slain;
> Nor bull nor lion shall avail
> The foe's fierce onset to restrain;
> Lo! onward moves his dark array,
> Mighty as Zeus, and will not stay
> Till King or city be his prey."

Remembering therefore this oracle, and desiring to get for the Spartans all the glory of this matter, Leonidas sent away the others. This is rather to be believed than that they had a controversy in the council, and so departed in an unseemly fashion and without order.

And that this was so is manifest both from other things and also from what befell Megistias the soothsayer. This Megistias was an Acarnanian and of the house, it was reported, of Melampus; and Leonidas would have sent him away together with the others, lest he should perish with them. Megistias indeed would not depart, but he sent away his son who chanced to be with the army; for indeed he had no other son but him only.

The others thereupon hearkened to the words of Leonidas and departed; but the Thespians and the Thebans only abode with the Spartans. This the Thebans indeed did against their will, for Leonidas kept these to be as hostages; but the Thespians remained of their own free will, affirming that they would not leave Leonidas and his companions. Wherefore they abode in the Pass and perished together with the Spartans. Their leader was Demophilus.

CHAPTER XIV

OF THE BATTLE OF THERMOPYLÆ *(continued)*

So soon as the sun was risen Xerxes made libations; and about the time when the market begins to fill he commanded that the army should advance. This he had been bidden to do by Ephialtes, because the way for them that descended the mountain was shorter by far than the way for them that ascended. Now when the Persians were seen to approach, Leonidas and his companions, as knowing that their end was near, went further than they had gone on the days before into that part which is broader. For before they had been wont to guard the wall, and advancing therefrom to fight in the narrows of the Pass. But now they joined battle with the barbarians in the open space, slaying great multitudes of them. As for these indeed the captains of their companies standing behind them and having great whips, drave them forward. And many were thrust into the sea by the press and so perished; and many were trodden down by their companions. Nor did any one take any count of them that perished. And the Greeks, knowing that death was at hand, now that the barbarians had come round over the mountains, recked not of their lives, but fought with rage that was beyond all measure. By this time the spears of the greater part were already broken, so that they smote down the Persians with their swords. While they thus fought King Leonidas was slain, having done many deeds of valor; and there fell many other Spartans with him, men of renown. Many famous Persians also were slain at this time, and among them were two sons of Darius. And there was an exceeding fierce fight between the Spartans and Persians concerning the body of Leonidas; but in the end the Spartans prevailed, so great was their valor, and carried it away, and they drave back the Persians four times. But when the Greeks perceived that the Persians that followed Ephialtes were at hand, they returned to the narrows of the Pass, beyond the wall, and gathered themselves together in the company on the mound that is at the entering in of the Pass, where in aftertime there was set a lion of stone over the grave of King Leonidas. Here such as had swords yet remaining to them unbroken, defended themselves with them; and the rest fought with their hands and teeth, till at the last the barbarians, some pulling down the walls and assailing them in front and others surrounding them on every side, overwhelmed them with stones and arrows and the like.

All the Spartans and Thespians showed themselves right valiant; but the bravest of all was Dieneces a Spartan. It was this Dieneces that spake a very noteworthy saying before the Spartans joined battle with the Persians. And the saying was this. A man of Trachis affirmed that when the Persians shot off their arrows the sun was darkened by the number of them. But Dieneces was not one whit astonished at the matter, but, taking no heed at all of the multitude of the Persians, made answer, saying, "This is good news that the stranger from Trachis brings us, for if the Persians so hide the sun then shall we fight in the shade." Many such like sayings did this Dieneces speak. Next after this Dieneces were two brothers, Alpheus and Maron; and of the Thespians the bravest was one Dithyrambus.

All these were buried even where they were slain. On them that died before that Leonidas had sent away a part of his army, there was written this epitaph—

> "Four times a thousand men from Pelops' land
> Three thousand times a thousand did withstand."

But over the Spartans by themselves there was written—

> "Go, tell the Spartans, thou that passest by,
> That here, obedient to their laws, we lie."

And over the soothsayer was this—

> "Here lies the great Megistias, whom of yore
> The Persian host, from swift Asopus shore
> Ascending, slew. The seer his doom could read,
> Yet left not Sparta's chieftains in their need."

The other columns indeed and that which was written upon them did the Amphictyons set up; but the column of Megistias the seer and the inscription thereon Simonides set up for friendship's sake.

Of the three hundred two, Eurytus and Aristodemus,

were absent from their companions on the day of the battle. Now these two might, if they had been willing to agree, either have returned both of them to Sparta, for Leonidas had sent them away from the army and they lay at Alpeni, grievously afflicted with sickness of the eyes, or if they were not willing so to return, have died along with the others. As for Eurytus, when he knew that the Persians had come round by the path, he called for his arms and put them on him, and bade his helot lead him into the battle. So the helot led him to the battle, and then turned and fled, and Eurytus thrust himself into the press of the battle, and so perished. But as for Aristodemus his courage failed him, and he tarried at Alpeni. Now if Aristodemus only had been sick and so returned alive to Sparta, or if they two had so returned together, it may well be believed that the Spartans would have had no indignation against them; but seeing that, both being in the same case, one perished but the other was not willing to die, it could not but be that they should have great indignation against him that still lived.

Such is the story that some tell about Aristodemus; but others say that having been sent as a messenger from the army, when he might have returned before the battle, he lingered on the way of set purpose, but that his fellow messenger returned and was slain. This Aristodemus, going back to Sparta, was held in great shame and dishonor. For no Spartan would give him fire, nor would any talk with him, but they called him "Aristodemus the Coward." Notwithstanding at the battle of Platæa he did away with all his disgrace.

As for the Thebans that were with Leonidas, for a while they fought together with the other Greeks against the Persians, doing this by compulsion. But when the barbarians prevailed, and the Greeks gathered themselves together at the mound, then the Thebans separated themselves from them, and stretching forth their hands came near to the barbarians, and cried, speaking indeed the veriest truth, that they had yielded themselves to the Persians, and had given earth and water to the King, none sooner, and that they had come to Thermopylæ under compulsion, and were without guilt for the loss that had befallen the King's army. Thus they were saved alive, and indeed they had the Thessalians to witness for them that they spake the truth. Nevertheless they were not altogether fortunate, for some of them were slain by the barbarians as they approached, and the others were branded with the King's mark, for such was the command of Xerxes. The first that suffered this was their general Leontiades. The son of this Leontiades, Eurymachus, was afterward slain by the men of Platæa when he came with four hundred other Thebans seeking to take their city.

These things being finished, the King sent for Demaratus and spake to him, saying, "Demaratus, thou art a good man, as I know by thy speaking of the truth, for indeed all things have turned out according to thy saying. Tell me now how many in number are the Spartans that yet remain? and how many of them are such as they that have now fought against us?"

Then said Demaratus, "O King, there are many Lacedæmonians; but in this country of Lacedæmon there is a certain city, Sparta, wherein are, as near as may be, eight thousand men as brave as them that fought in the Pass. The other Lacedæmonians are not a match for these; nevertheless they are brave men."

Xerxes said, "Tell me now, Demaratus, how shall we best get the mastery over these men? Speak, for thou wast a King among them and must need know all their counsels."

Demaratus made answer, "Since thou seekest counsel of me so earnestly, O King, I will tell thee, as is right, the best thing thou canst do. Send three hundred of thy ships against the land of the Lacedæmonians. Now there lieth over against this land a certain island, Cythera, concerning which island one Chilon, a very wise man that once dwelt among us, was wont to say that it would be far better for the Spartans that it should be sunk under the sea than that it should be above the sea. This he said because he feared always lest some such thing should be done as I am now about to tell thee. And he said it knowing nothing of thy coming against Greece, but fearing all coming of strangers to this place. Send men therefore to this island, and let them harass the Spartans from thence. And it shall be that if they have a war of their own close at home they will not be a trouble to thee, so as to help the other Greeks when thy army seeks to subdue them. And when thou hast subdued the rest of Greece, the Spartans, being left alone, will be feeble. But if thou wilt not follow this counsel then know that there shall come to pass that which I now tell thee. When thou comest to the Peloponnesus thou wilt find a narrow neck of land; and at this neck all the men of the Peloponnesus that are leagued together against thee will be gathered together, and there wilt thou have to fight battles fiercer by far than that which thou hast now seen."

Now it so chanced that Achæmenes, who was brother to King Xerxes, and had command of the fleet, was present when Demaratus thus spake. Fearing then that the King might follow this counsel, he brake in, "I see, O King, that thou listenest to the counsels of a man that envies thy good fortune, and seeks to betray thee. This indeed is ever the manner of the Greeks; they envy good fortune, and hate that which is stronger than themselves. If now, when we have lost four hundred ships by shipwreck, three hundred more shall be sent away from the fleet to sail round the Peloponnesus, then will our enemies be a match for us. But if we keep our whole fleet together, then will it be such as they will not dare to encounter. Consider also that if that which we have on the land and that which we have on the sea advance together, the one will be able to help the other. But if thou part them asunder, the fleet will not be able to help thee, nor thou to help the fleet. Only order thine own affairs well, and take no thought about thine enemies, whether they will join battle with thee, or what they will do, or how many they be in number. Surely they without us can manage their own affairs and we ours without them. As to the Spartans, if they come out to fight against us, they will in no wise heal this great wound that they have now received at our hands."

To this the King made answer, "This is well said,

Achæmenes, and I will follow thy counsel. For though Demaratus saith what he deems the best for me, his judgment is worse than thine. But this I will not believe, that he has not good will for me and my fortunes. So much I know from the counsel that he has given me before, and also from his own affairs. For that a man may envy a fellow-citizen that is more fortunate than he, and may hate him secretly, and if he be asked for counsel will not speak the thing that is best, is to be believed, unless indeed he be of a very rare and excellent virtue. But a friend rejoices in the prosperity of a friend that is of another country, and gives him counsel according to the best of his power. Now this Demaratus is my friend, and I warn all men that hereafter they keep themselves from speaking evil of him."

When Xerxes had thus spoken, he went to see the bodies of them that had been slain. And when he came to the body of Leonidas, knowing him to have been the captain and King of the Spartans, he commanded that they should cut the head from it and put it on a cross, which may be taken for a proof that there was no man that Xerxes hated so much as he hated Leonidas while he was yet alive; for else he had not done this dishonor to his dead body. For the Persians are wont, for the most part, more than other men, to show honor to them that have shown themselves good men in war.

It must yet be told how the Spartans first knew that the King had it in his mind to bring an army against Greece. This Demaratus, of whom mention has been made, was not friendly, it would appear, to them that had driven him forth. Wherefore it may be doubted whether he did this thing that shall now be told from goodwill or from insolence. So soon as Xerxes had fixed it in his mind to march against Greece, Demaratus, being then in the city of Susa, and hearing the matter, desired to send tidings of it to the Spartans. And the way which he devised of sending them was this, for there was great peril lest he should be discovered. This therefore was his contrivance. He took a tablet that had two leaves, and having cleared away from it the wax, he wrote upon the wood the purpose of the King. And having done this he melted the wax again over the writing, knowing that the guards of the road would not trouble themselves about a tablet that was seen to be empty. But when the tablet was brought to Sparta no one could understand the matter, till Gorgo, that was daughter to Cleomenes and wife to Leonidas, discovered it to them, for she said, "Scrape the wax from off the tablet and you will of a surety find writing upon the wood." Thus did the Spartans hear of the coming of the King, and forthwith sent tidings of it to the other Greeks.

CHAPTER XV

OF THE SHIPS OF THE GREEKS AT ARTEMISIUM

THE Greeks had in all two hundred and seventy and one ships of war having three banks of oars, and of smaller ships a few. Of these the Athenians furnished one hundred and twenty and seven, certain of these being manned by the men of Platæa, who, though they had no knowledge of the seaman's art, yet of their valor and zeal took their part in the business. Also the Athenians supplied twenty ships to the men of Chalcis. The Spartans sent ten ships only; nevertheless, the commander of the fleet was a Spartan, Eurybiades by name, for the allies had said, "Unless a Spartan be commander we will break up the fleet, for an Athenian we will not serve."

Now there had been talk, even before the sending of the ambassadors to Sicily for help, how that it would be well to hand over to the Athenians the command of the fleet. But when the allies set themselves against the thing, then the Athenians gave place, for they desired above all things that Greece should be saved, and judged, and that right truly, that if there should be a strife

136

concerning the preeminence, it would surely perish. And indeed a strife between kindred is as much worse than war, wherein all have one mind, as war itself is worse than peace. The Athenians, knowing this, did not hold out for themselves, but gave place. Only afterward, when the occasion served, they showed their thoughts. For when the Greeks had driven back the Persians, so that they had now to fight for their own country, then finding occasion in the insolence of Pausanias, they took away the chief command from the Spartans. But this happened afterward.

When the Greeks that assembled at Artemisium saw the ships of the barbarians how many in number they were, and how the whole country was filled with their armament, and saw that the Persians had prospered in their undertaking beyond what they had thought, they were in great fear, and took counsel together whether they should not depart from Artemisium and betake themselves to the inner parts of their country. Now when the men of Eubœa were ware that the Greeks had such a purpose in their minds, they came to Eurybiades, and besought him to remain a while, till they should have removed their children and their slaves to a place of safety. And when they could not persuade Eurybiades they departed from him and went to Themistocles, the commander of the Athenians, and persuaded him to do this thing, giving him thirty talents of silver. And the manner in which Themistocles caused the Greeks to tarry at Artemisium was this. First he sent to Eurybiades five talents of the thirty, making as though they came from himself. Thus was Eurybiades persuaded. Then to Adeimantus of Corinth—for this man still opposed, affirming that he would sail away from Artemisium and would by no means tarry—he said with an oath, "Surely thou wilt not forsake us. I will give thee greater gifts if thou abide with us than the King would give thee for going over to him." And when he had said this he sent three talents to the Corinthian's ship. Thus these two were won over by gifts, and the men of Eubœa had what they desired. As for Themistocles, he made no small gain in this matter, for he kept that which was left for himself, none knowing of it. They that had a share in the money believed that it had been sent from Athens for this very end. Thus did it come to pass that the Greeks fought with the barbarians at Artemisium.

As for the battle, it was in this wise. When the barbarians saw that the ships of the Greeks were few in number they were desirous to fight without delay, hoping that they might take them before they could escape, and fearing lest they should flee. But they judged it better not to sail straight against them, lest the Greeks seeing them so advance should take to flight, for that if night should fall while they fled they would clean escape out of their hands. Now the desire of the Persians was that not even the torchbearer, as men say, should escape. (When the Spartans go forth to war they have with them one who keeps the sacred fire for the sacrifices. Him they defend with all their might; nor is he killed unless the whole army perish.) They contrived therefore this plan. They separated two hundred ships from the whole fleet, and sent them around the island of Eubœa, commanding them to make a very wide circuit, lest the Greeks should see them. And their purpose was that the two hundred ships should bar the way by the Euripus (the Euripus is the channel at the extremity of the island southward), and that so the Greeks might be shut in on either side, for the two hundred ships would be behind them, and the remainder of the fleet would attack them from before. Having so done they remained in their place, till they should know by a signal that the two hundred ships had accomplished their voyage.

Now there was among the Persians a certain Scyllias of Scione, than whom there was in those days no more skillful diver. This man had saved much treasure for the Persians after the great storm that fell on the fleet from Mount Pelion, getting also no small portion for himself. He had been minded for some time to go over to the Greeks, but had not before found occasion. And indeed how he passed from the Persians to the Greeks is not certainly known; but marvelous things are told about it. For some say that diving into the sea at Aphetæ he did not come up to the top of the water so much as once till he was arrived at Artemisium, so passing through eighty furlongs of sea or thereabouts. Many other things are told about this man that are manifestly false, and some that are true. But as to his coming from Aphetæ to Artemisium, doubtless he came in a boat. And so soon as he was come he told the commanders of the fleet of the damage done to the Persians, and also of the two hundred ships that had been sent round Eubœa.

When the commanders heard these things they took counsel what they should do. At the first they proposed to remain in their place till midnight, and then sail to meet the two hundred ships; but afterward, changing their purpose, they set sail, not long after noonday, toward the fleet of the barbarians, desiring to make a trial of their manner of fighting and of their skill.

Now when the Persians perceived the Greeks thus sailing against them, and saw how few ships they had, they thought that they were mad, and went out to meet them, not doubting that they should easily take them all; for their ships were many more in number and also sailed better. And such of the Ionians as wished well to the Greeks, and served with the Persians against their will, were much troubled to see the fleet of the Greeks surrounded, thinking it certain that none of them would escape; but they that had no love for the Greeks rejoiced, and strove with each other who should first take an Athenian ship, and gain for himself great gifts from the King. For the Athenians were most accounted of both among the Persians and the Greeks.

The Greeks, when the first signal was given, brought the sterns of their ships together and turned their prows toward their enemies; and on the second signal they joined battle; and though they were shut into a narrow space they bare themselves bravely and took twenty ships of the barbarians, and with them Philaon, brother to Gorgus King of Salamis, a man held in much respect. And the first of the Greeks that took a ship of the Persians was Lycomedes of Athens, to whom was given the prize of valor. But while they still fought, and victory was yet doubtful, the night fell. So the Greeks sailed back to their place, and the Persians also, marveling much at what had befallen them, for it was far otherwise than what they had hoped. In this battle one only of the Greeks came over from the Persians to the Greeks, a man of Lesbos, to whom the Athenians gave afterward certain lands in Salamis for a reward.

But before night a great rain, with thunder and lightning from Mount Pelion, fell upon the Persians; and the dead corpses of them that had been slain in the battle, and broken pieces of the ships, were floated into the midst of the ships and hindered the oars. And the Persians were greatly afraid, thinking that there was no end of their perils, first the storm, and then the battle, and now this great storm of rain. But as for them that were sent round the island they fared much worse, for the storm fell upon them while they were in the open sea. They were near to the Hollows of Eubœa when the wind and the rain overtook them; nor could they hold up against the storm, but being driven they knew not whither, fell among rocks, and so were utterly destroyed. Thus did the Gods contrive that the number of the Persian ships should be made equal to the number of the ships of the Greeks.

Right glad were the barbarians when the morning was come; and that day they tarried in their place, being well content to be quiet after all their troubles. And to the Greeks there came fifty and three ships of the Athenians. Tidings also were brought how that all the ships of the barbarians that had sought to sail round Eubœa had perished by reason of the storm. All this put them in good heart; and at the same hour at which they had sailed the day before, they went forth and fell on some Cilician ships and destroyed them, and so, at nightfall, sailed back to Artemisium.

The third day the barbarians took it much to heart that so few ships of the Greeks should work them such injury. They feared also what Xerxes would do to them; therefore they did not tarry till the Greeks should begin the battle, but bidding each other be of good heart, about noonday they sailed out. Now it so fell out that these three days were the very days on which the Persians and the Greeks had fought in the Pass. For the Greeks at Artemisium sought to keep the Euripus even as Leonidas and his comrades sought to keep the Pass. So the Greeks strengthened each other, saying that they should not suffer the barbarians to go from thence into their land, and the Persians were fain to destroy the fleet of their enemies and so get the mastery of the strait. This day then the barbarians set themselves in order of battle and sailed against the Greeks, and these kept in their place at Artemisium. But when the Persians, having their ships in the shape of a crescent, made as if they would take the Greeks on both sides, then these sailed out and joined battle. This day neither the one nor the other had the upper hand, for the fleet of Xerxes was damaged not a little by reason of the multitude of the ships, these falling into confusion and striking the one against the other; nevertheless it held out and gave no place to the enemy, for the Persians counted it a grievous thing that they should be put to flight by a few. Thus it came to pass that many of the ships of the Greeks were broken, and many of the men perished. But of the barbarians there perished more by a great many both of ships and of men. And after they had fought together for a long time they parted asunder, going right gladly to their own place. In this battle of all the men of Xerxes none bare themselves more bravely than the Egyptians, and of all the Greeks none more than the Athenians, and among these than Cleinias the son of Alcibiades. This Cleinias served at his own charges, having two hundred men and his own ship.

CHAPTER XVI

OF THE DEPARTURE OF THE GREEKS FROM ARTEMISIUM AND OF THE ADVANCE OF XERXES

THE battle being ended, the Greeks got possession of the broken ships and of the dead bodies of the slain; but seeing that they had been roughly handled, the Athenians not less than the others—for the half of their ships had suffered damage—they purposed to depart. Then Themistocles, thinking that if he could divide the men of Ionia and the men of Caria from the barbarians, the Greeks could have the mastery of the rest, gathered together the commanders, while the Eubœans were driving down their sheep to the sea, and told them that he had conceived a device by which he could divide from the King the bravest of his allies. Also he said that they should kill as many as they would of the sheep of the Eubœans, for that it was better that they should have them than that they should fall into the hands of the barbarians; also he would have the camp-fire according to custom. "And I will take care," he said, "that you shall get back to Greece without any damage."

Now the people of Eubœa had paid no regard to the oracle of Bacis, making light of it altogether, and neither removing their goods from the island, nor yet putting them into their strong places. And the oracle was this:

> Ye sons of fair Eubœa heed:
> Whene'er the strangers' dark array
> Shall bridge the sea with ropes of reed,
> Drive ye your bleating flocks away.

And by this neglect they were brought to ruin.

By this time there was come a messenger from Thermopylæ. For the Greeks had set a man in Trachis to tell them that fought in the Pass how it fared with the ships at Artemisium, and there was another man with King Leonidas who was to bring news to Artemisium of the doings of the Spartans. This man was now come, telling all that had befallen the Greeks in the Pass; which when the commanders of the fleet had heard, they delayed no longer, but departed, each in their order, first the Corinthians, and last of all the Athenians. But Themistocles chose the swiftest of the Athenian ships, and going to the places for watering, engraved there upon the rocks certain words which the Ionians coming the next day to Artemisium read. And the words were these, "Men of Ionia, ye do wrong making war against your fathers and seeking to enslave the land of Greece. Of right ye should be on our side. But if this be not possible to you, yet stand ye aloof from the battle, and entreat the Carians also that they do likewise. And if so be that ye can not either help us or stand aloof, being under such constraint that ye cannot revolt against the barbarians, yet, when the battle is joined, ye should hold your hands, remembering that ye are of our blood, and that for your sake we first provoked the barbarians to wrath." For Themistocles said to himself, "Either this writing will not come to the knowledge of the King, and the Ionians will perchance be persuaded to help us; or, coming to his knowledge, it will cause him to have doubts of them, and he will not suffer them to come into battle together with his ships."

Now when the barbarians heard that the Greeks had fled from Artemisium, at the first they would not believe it, but afterward, finding it to be so, they sailed thither. And when they were arrived at the place there came a herald from King Xerxes, saying, "Comrades, the King permits any that will to leave his place and see for himself how he fights against the foolish men that thought to resist his might." But before that he sent the herald he had ordered matters in this wise. He took of them that had been slain of his army at the Pass one thousand (but the number of the whole was twenty thousand), and left them to be seen; but the rest he hid away, digging two great trenches for them and covering them with leaves, and heaping earth upon them. Now when the herald had made this proclamation there could scarcely be found a boat, so many desired to see the sight. So they crossed over and saw it, passing among the dead bodies; all these they thought to be either Spartans or men of Thespiæ, though indeed there were many helots among the slain. Nevertheless they that crossed over perceived what Xerxes had done with the dead of his own army. And indeed it was a foolish device, for on the one side were to be seen the thousand men, and on the other four thousand, gathered together all of them into one place. This day therefore they spent in this fashion, and the next the seamen went back to their ships and Xerxes with his army went forward.

About this time there came to the Persians certain men from Arcadia, poor men that sought for a livelihood. When these were brought before the King, one of the Persians asked them, saying, "What do the Greeks at this season?" The Arcadians answered, "They hold the games at Olympia, looking on the sports and on the races of chariots." Then said the Persian, "What is the prize for which they contend?" And when the Arcadians answered, "They contend for a wreath of olive leaves," Tritantæchmes, that was the son to Artabanus, cried out, "Now, by the Gods, O Mardonius, what manner of men are these against whom thou bringest us, that they contend with each other, not for money, but for glory only?" This was in truth a noble thing that he said, but it angered the King, so that he charged Tritantæchmes with cowardice.

From Trachis the Persians marched into Doris, and from Doris into Phocis. This they laid waste, burning the towns and the temples. As for the Phocians themselves, they escaped, for the most part, with their wives and children, to the heights of Mount Parnassus. When they had passed through the land of Phocis the barbarians divided their army into two parts, whereof the one, with King Xerxes, marched toward Athens through the land of Bœotia, and the other, having taken to themselves guides, marched toward the temple at Delphi. This they did purposing to spoil the temple, and to bring the treasure to the King; and indeed the King knew all the notable things that were laid up in the treasury at Delphi better than he knew the things that he had left in his own house; for there was continually much talk about them, and especially about the offerings which Crœsus, King of the Lydians, had made to the god.

The men of Delphi, when they knew of the coming of the Persians, were in great fear; therefore they inquired of the oracle what they should do with the treasures of the temple, whether they should bury them in the earth, or take them away to some other land. But the god answered them in these words, "Move them not, for I am sufficient to defend that which is mine own." When the men of Delphi heard these words, they took counsel about themselves. First they carried their women and children across the gulf of Corinth to the land of Achaia, and after that they fled, for the most part, to the heights of Parnassus, and their goods they hid in the Corycian cave; but some of them escaped to Amphissa, a city of the Locrians; of all the men of Delphi there were left in the city sixty only, and the prophet.

So soon as the barbarians were come near so that they could see the temple, the prophet (his name was Acetatus) espied the holy arms which it is not lawful for a man to touch, lying without the temple. And while he went to tell this marvel to them that were in the city, and the barbarians were coming up with all speed, and were now near to the temple of Athene, there befell marvels greater by far than that which has been told. A great marvel indeed is it that arms should move of their own accord so as to be seen lying without the temple, but the things that befell afterward are greater by far, and such indeed that nothing can be compared with them. First of all, so soon as the barbarians, coming up the road, were now hard by the temple of Athene, there fell on them great thunderbolts from heaven, and two great rocks brake off from the top of Mount Parnassus, and rolled down upon them with a great crash, and slew many of them, and there was heard also from the temple a war-cry and a shout of victory. And when the barbarians saw and heard all these things, great fear came upon them, so that they turned their backs and fled. And when the men of Delphi perceived that they fled, they came down and pursued after them, and slew not a few of them. And they that escaped fled into Bœotia, turning neither to the right hand nor to the left. They said also that, over and above the other marvels that have been told, they saw two men at arms, whose stature exceeded the stature of a man, following after them and slaying them. These two men the men of Delphi affirm to have been heroes of the country, Phylacus and Autonous. These two have each a temple and a precinct near to the city of Delphi. As for the rocks that fell from Parnassus, they are to be seen to this day in the precinct of Athene, in which they lodged after that they had passed through the host of the barbarians.

CHAPTER XVII

OF THE GREEKS AT SALAMIS AND OF THE CITY OF ATHENS

THE ships of the Greeks, having departed from Artemisium, came to Salamis. The Athenians had besought them to do this that they might carry their women and children out of their country, and might also take counsel together what was best to be done. For indeed things had not happened according to their expectations. For they had thought to find the men of the Peloponnese drawn up with their whole force in the land of Bœotia to do battle with the barbarians. But now they heard that these purposed to build a wall across the Isthmus, and so defend their own country, suffering the rest of Greece to take thought for itself. And this the Greeks did. And so soon as they were come thither there flowed to them no small force that had been gathered together at Pogon, the haven of the Trœzenians. For the word had gone forth that all who would fight for Greece should be gathered together at Pogon. All these the same Euribiades that was at Artemisium commanded, being a Spartan but not of the house of the Kings. Of all the ships the best were the ships of the Athenians, being in number one hundred and eighty. These were now altogether manned by their own people, for the men of Platæa had gone to carry away their wives and children from their city. The men of Ægina sent thirty ships, leaving certain others to defend their city. From the island of Naxos there came four. These indeed had been sent by their people to help the Persians, but they made light of the command and helped the Greeks. This they did at the instance of Democritus, a notable man among the Naxians and captain of a ship. The men of Seriphos and Siphnos and Melos also helped the Greeks, being the only islanders that had not given earth and water to the barbarians. These three sent in all four ships of fifty oars. And of all the countries beyond the sea the men of Crotona only came to the help of the Greeks in their great peril. These sent one ship which Phayllus, a man that had been crowned at the Pythian games, commanded. Now the number of the ships in all was three hundred and seventy and eight; but in this number the ships of fifty oars were not reckoned.

Meanwhile there had been made a proclamation among the Athenians that each man should save his children and his household as best he could. The most part sent them away to Trœzen; but some sent them to Ægina, and some to Salamis. This they did with all speed, desiring to obey the words of the oracle, and also for another reason which shall now be told. The Athenians say that in their citadel in the temple there dwells a great snake that is the guardian of the place. And indeed they set out for this snake a monthly provision of food, as for a veritable creature; and the monthly provision is a honey cake. This honey cake which before had always been eaten, was now seen to be untouched. When the priestess told these things to the people they were more earnest than before to leave the city, as thinking that the goddess Athene had deserted the citadel. Nevertheless they did not all depart, for the Persians, when they came, found the city indeed desolate of inhabitants, but in the citadel certain men, that were either ministers of the temple or of the poorer sort that for lack of means had not departed with the rest of the people to Salamis. But some of them went not, thinking that they rightly understood the oracle of the Pythia when she said, "The wooden wall shall not be taken;" for that by this wall was signified, not the ships, but a veritable wall of wood. These therefore had fenced about the citadel with doors and pieces of wood, and so awaited the coming of the Persians.

The Persians indeed encamped on the hill that is over against the citadel (this hill the Athenians call the hill of Ares) and began the siege, shooting at the Greeks arrows with burning tow upon them that so they might set fire to the barricade. Nevertheless the men held out, though indeed they were in evil case, and their wooden wall had failed them; nor would they hearken to the words of the sons of Pisistratus when these would have them surrender, but they rolled down great stones upon the barbarians as these came up to the gates, and so kept the place. And for many days Xerxes was in great doubt, and knew not how he should prevail over them; but at last they discovered a way of access. For it must needs be that the oracle should be fulfilled, that all the country of the Athenians upon the mainland should be conquered by the barbarians. Certain Persians climbed up the hill where there was no watch, no one believing that any man could mount by that way, so steep was it. (The place is on the face of the cliff, behind the gates and the way by which men commonly ascend.) So soon as the Athenians saw them now already on the top, some threw themselves from the wall and so perished; and some fled for refuge to the sanctuary. But the Persians, when they had opened the gates of the citadel for their fellows, slew all them that had taken sanctuary; and afterward they plundered the temple and burned all the citadel with fire. Then Xerxes, being now wholly master of Athens, sent off a messenger, a horseman, to Artabanus, to tell him of his good success. Also, on the second day after the sending of the herald, he commanded the Athenian exiles that had followed in his train to go up to the citadel and do sacrifice in the place according to the custom of their country. This he did either by reason of a dream, or because it repented him that he had burned the temple. And the exiles did as the King commanded. And when they were come to the citadel they found a marvelous thing. There was in the citadel a temple of Erectheus, whom the Athenians call the "earth-born," and in the temple an olive tree, which Athene left for a memorial of her when she contended with Poseidon for the land of the Athenians. Now this olive had been burned with other things in the temple, but when the Athenians went up, according to the King's commandment, they found that there had sprung forth from the trunk a fresh shoot of a cubit in length.

So soon as tidings came to the Greeks of Salamis of the things that had befallen Athens and its citadel, there came upon them such fear that some of the captains would not wait till the council should have voted, but embarked in their vessels with all haste, and hoisted up their sails, as though they would fly without delay. And such as staid at the council voted that the fleet should give battle to the Persians at the Isthmus. Afterward, it being now night, the captains departed, each man to his own vessel.

And when Themistocles was come to his ship there met him a certain Mnesiphilus, an Athenian, who asked him what the council had decreed. And when Themistocles said, "They have decreed that we should sail to the Isthmus, and there fight for the Peloponnese," Mnesiphilus made answer, "If these men take away their ships from Salamis, there will be no one country for which ye may fight. For the Greeks will depart each to his own city, and neither Eurybiades nor any other man shall be able to hinder them from so scattering themselves. So shall Greece perish by the folly of their children. If therefore there be any device by which thou canst deliver us from this end, haste and make trial of it. Happily thou mayest persuade Eurybiades to change his purpose and remain in this place."

This counsel pleased Themistocles well. To Mnesiphilus indeed he answered nothing, but he went straightway to the ship of Eurybiades, and said that he had a matter concerning the common weal about which he would speak with him. Then said Eurybiades, "Come into my ship if thou hast aught to say." So Themistocles sat by his side and told him all that he had heard from Mnesiphilus—only he said these things as if from himself—and added also many other things. So urgent was he that at the last Eurybiades went forth and gathered together the other captains to council. So soon then as these were gathered together, before that Eurybiades had set forth the matter wherefore they were assembled, Themistocles, as one that was wholly intent on his purpose, said many things, so that Adeimantus of Corinth cried out to him, "Themistocles, in the games they that start too soon are scourged." "Yea," said Themistocles, excusing himself, "but they that linger are not crowned." Thus he answered the Corinthian softly. And to Eurybiades he spake, not indeed after his former manner, how that the ships would be scattered from where he should have sailed to the Isthmus, for the allies were present, and he thought it not seemly to say this thing in their ears, but rather in some such fashion as this: "It is in thy hands to save Greece, if thou wilt hearken unto me and abide in this place, and so give battle to the barbarians, not heeding those who would have thee depart hence to the Isthmus with thy ships. For hear now, and set these two things one against the other. If the host give battle at the Isthmus, then shall we fight in the open sea, than which there could be nothing less to our advantage, seeing that our ships are fewer in number and these heavier. Also we shall lose Salamis and Megara and

Ægina, though we prosper in the battle. For remember that the army of the barbarians will follow, together with their fleet, and that thou wilt thus bring both the one and the other to the Peloponnesus, and so put all Greece upon the hazard. But if thou wilt hearken unto me, see what we shall gain. First we shall do battle in a narrow space, a thing much to our advantage and to the harm of our enemies. And secondly, we shall yet keep Salamis, where we have put our wives and children, and Megara also and Ægina. And at Salamis, saith the oracle, we shall prevail over the barbarians."

When Themistocles had thus spoken, Adeimantus of Corinth reproached him again, bidding him be silent, because he was a man without a city (for Athens had been destroyed by the barbarians). Then Themistocles brake out against him and the Corinthians with many bitter words, and saying, "Nay, but we have a city and a land greater than yours, for we have two hundred ships well manned, whose attack no city of the Greeks would be able to withstand." Then he turned to Eurybiades, and said with all earnestness, "If thou wilt abide here and bear thyself bravely all will be well; but if not, then wilt thou bring Greece to ruin. For verily we will take our wives and children and go straightway to Siris in Italy, which is ours. Verily, when ye have lost our help, ye will remember what I have said this day."

When Eurybiades heard these words, he changed his purpose, knowing that if the Athenians should depart, the rest of the fleet should not be able to withstand the Persians. Wherefore he made his resolve that he would stay and give battle at Salamis. Then all the captains made ready for battle. After this, at daybreak there was an earthquake, and it seemed good to the Greeks to make supplications to the Gods, and to call the sons of Æacus to their help. And this they did, for they put up prayers, and sent a ship to Salamis to fetch Æacus and his children.

A certain Dicæus, an exile of Athens and a man of repute among the barbarians, told this tale of what he saw about this time. He chanced to be with Demaratus the Spartan in the plain of Thria, the land of Attica having been by this time laid waste by the army of Xerxes, and he saw coming from Eleusis a great cloud of dust, such as a host of thirty thousand men might make in their march. And while the two marveled who these could be that could cause such dust, he heard voices and the sound, as it seemed to him, of the hymn to Bacchus. Now Demaratus heard the voices, and asked what they were saying, for he knew nothing of the mysteries of Eleusis. Then said Dicæus, "O Demaratus, of a truth some great trouble will overtake the army of the King. For seeing that Attica is void of inhabitants, these that sing are surely gods, and they come from Eleusis to help the Athenians and their allies. If therefore this that we see turn to the Peloponnese, there will be peril to the King and to his army, but if to Salamis, then there will be peril to the fleet. For know that year by year the Athenians keep a feast to the Mother and Daughter, and the voices which thou heardst were singing the hymn of the feast." Then said Demaratus, "See that thou tell the matter to no man. For if the King hear it, thou wilt surely perish. Hold thou thy peace therefore; the Gods will order as they please with the army of the King."

By this time the ships of the barbarians were come to Phalerum, which is a haven of Athens. And it seemed good to Xerxes to learn the judgment of them that had command in the fleet. Wherefore he went on board and sat on a seat of honor, and all the kings and the captains sat before him, each in his place, after the pleasure of the King. The King of Sidon sat in the first place, and in the second the King of Tyre. Then Xerxes sent Mardonius, bidding him ask each in his order what he counseled, whether they should fight or no. To this all made answer in the same words that they should fight, save Artemisia of Halicarnassus only, who spake after this fashion, "Say to the King, O Mardonius, what I now say to thee. Seeing that I bare myself not less bravely than the others in the battles at the island of Eubœa, I have the right to speak what I judge to be most for thy advantage. I say then spare thy ships and fight not. These men are better than thine upon the sea, even as men are better than women. Art thou not master of Athens, for which thou camest hither? Doth any man resist thee? Or if thou art not yet satisfied, thou canst easily accomplish all that is in thine heart to do. These men will not long abide in their place, and indeed they have, I fear, no store of food in the island; and if thou goest forward toward the Peloponnese, they will be scattered each to his own city, for the men of the Peloponnese will not care to fight for the Athenians. But I fear me much that some great evil will befall thee, if thou art resolved to join battle with the Greeks by sea.

For remember that good masters have ever evil servants, and evil masters good servants; thou indeed art the best of men, but thy servants are evil. For these thy allies, as they are called, these men of Egypt and of Cyprus and of Cilicia and of Pamphylia, are of no account."

When Artemisia spake these words all that wished her well were much troubled, for they thought that she would surely be cruelly dealt with by the King, because she counseled him not to give battle; but all that were enemies to her rejoiced, and they that envied her for the honor which the King had done to her beyond all the allies, thinking that she would perish. Nevertheless Xerxes, when the words of all the kings and the captains were told to him, was not pleased with any so much as with the words of Artemisia. Nevertheless it seemed good to him to follow the counsel of the greater number, and to give battle; for he thought that the ships had not done their best at Eubœa because he himself had been absent, and was minded to see the battle that should now be fought with his own eyes.

So the ships of the barbarians sailed to Salamis and took their places, as they had been commanded, no man hindering them; for the Greeks, especially the men of the Peloponnese, were greatly troubled, fearing lest they should be shut up in Salamis while their own country was left without defense.

The same night the army of the barbarians went forwards to the Peloponnese. There indeed all things had been done that the Persians might not be able to come into the country. For so soon as there came the tidings how that Leonidas and his companions had fallen at the Pass, straightway the inhabitants assembled from their cities and pitched their camp at the Isthmus, their commander being Cleombrotus, who was brother to Leonidas. First they blocked up the way of Susa, that leads from Megara to Corinth; and afterwards they built a wall across the Isthmus. This work they wrought in a few days only, for there were many thousands of men, and they worked without ceasing either by night or by day. Now the nations that were gathered at the Isthmus were these: the Lacedæmonians, all the Arcadians, the Corinthians, the men of Elis, the men of Sicyon, and of Epidaurus, and Phlius, and of Trœzen, and of Hermione. But the other nations, as the Achæans and the Argives, came not to the Isthmus, nor gave help to the Greeks, but rather, if the truth is to be told, gave help to the Persians.

CHAPTER XVIII

OF THE BATTLE OF SALAMIS

MEANWHILE there was much doubt and fear among the Greeks at Salamis. For a time indeed the captains talked privately the one with the other, marveling at the ill counsel of Eurybiades that he left the Peloponnese without defense; but at the last their discontent brake forth, and the assembly was called together, in which many things were said to the same purpose as in the former assembly, some affirming that they ought to sail away to the Peloponnese that they might defend it, it being a vain thing, they said, to remain at Salamis and fight for that which was already in the power of their enemies, and the men of Athens and of Ægina and of Megara being urgent that they should remain and give battle.

Then Themistocles, perceiving that his counsel should not prevail against the counsel of the men of the Peloponnese, went out secretly from the assembly, and sent straightway a messenger in a boat to the camp of the Persians. (The name of the messenger was Sicinnus, he was servant to Themistocles and tutor to his children; and after the war Themistocles caused him to become a citizen of Thespiæ, for the Thespians were admitting strangers to citizenship, and gave him great riches.) This Sicinnus therefore, going in a boat to the camp of the barbarians, spake to their captains, saying, "The commander of the Athenians has sent me, without the knowledge of the rest of the Greeks, to say that the Greeks are in great fear and purpose to fly from their place, and that ye have a great occasion of destroying them utterly, if only ye will not suffer them to escape. For indeed they are not of one mind, nor will they withstand you any more, but ye will see them fighting the one against the other, they that are on your side being opposed to them that are against you. And this my master does because he is a friend to the King, and because he would rather that you should prevail than that the Greeks should have the mastery."

When Sicinnus had thus spoken he departed straightway. And the Persians, because they believed what Sicinnus had told them, first landed many of their men on Psyttaleia, which is a little island between Salamis and the mainland; and next, about midnight, they moved the westernmost wing of their ships to Salamis, and those that were posted at Ceos and Cynosura set sail also, and filled all the strait even as far as Munychia. This they did that the Greeks might not be able to escape, but might be shut up within Salamis, and so pay the penalty of what they had done at Artemisium. As for the landing of the Persians at Psyttaleia, it was done for this cause, that when the battle was joined, and the broken ships and shipwrecked men should be carried down by the current to the island—which must needs be the case, seeing that it was in the very way of the battle that should be fought—these soldiers might be able to save their friends and slay their enemies. All this the barbarians did in silence, lest haply the Greeks should hear of the thing that had been done. So the Persians made ready for the battle, taking no rest, but toiling through all the night.

Meanwhile there was much angry talk among the captains at Salamis, for they knew not yet that they were shut in by the barbarians. But while they were assembled there came over from Ægina a certain Aristides, a man of Athens, that had been banished by the people (yet was he the best and most righteous man in Athens). This Aristides, coming to the council, would have Themistocles called out to speak with him. Now Themistocles was no friend to Aristides, but an enemy and very bitter against him; nevertheless, for the great trouble that had come upon the land, he took no count of this enmity, but came and called for him, wishing to speak with him. And when Themistocles was come forth, Aristides said to him, "We two, O Themistocles, have contended together aforetime concerning other things, but now let us contend who shall do the better service to his country. What I am now come to say is this: Let the men of the Peloponnese say little or say much about sailing hence, it is all one. For I affirm, of my own knowledge, that the Corinthians and Eurybiades himself cannot now depart, if they would, for that the barbarians have closed us in. But go thou and tell this thing to the captains." And Themistocles made answer, "This is good news thou hast brought, telling of your own knowledge the things that I greatly desired should come to pass. What the barbarians have done was indeed of my doing, because if the Greeks would not fight of their free will there was a necessity that they should be made to fight against their will. But as thou hast brought good news, tell it to the captains thyself, for if I tell it they will deem that I am lying to them. Tell it therefore thyself, and if they believe thee, well; but if not, yet can they not escape, if, as thou sayest, the Persians have closed us in."

Then Aristides went in to the assembly and told them that he was come from Ægina, having barely escaped the watch ships of the barbarians; and that they were closed in by the Persians. And he counseled them to make ready for the battle. Having so spoken he departed. Then there arose a great disputing, the greater part of the captains not believing these tidings. But while they doubted there came a ship of war from Tenos, which a certain Panætius commanded. This man told them the whole truth of the matter. For this cause the men of Tenos were written on the offering among them that destroyed the barbarians. And now the number of the ships of the Greeks was made up to three hundred and eighty.

The Greeks, learning that the words of the men of Tenos were true, made themselves ready for battle. And when it was morning there was called an assembly of the crews, and Themistocles spake to them very noble words, how that men should always choose good rather than evil, and honorable things rather than base things. When he had ended his speech he bade them embark on their ships; and while they were embarking there came from Ægina the ships that brought the children of Æacus. Then all the Greeks began to move their ships from their place. But so soon as they began to move them the Persians advanced against them, and the Greeks backed their oars, so that they would have beached the ships, only one Ameinias, a man of Athens, bade his men row forward, and coming forth before the line, drave his ship against a ship of the barbarians. Then others went to the help of Ameinias, and so the battle was begun. This is what the Athenians say; but the men of Ægina affirm that the ship that went to fetch the children of Æacus first began the battle. Also this story is told, that there was seen the likeness of a woman who cried with a loud voice, so that all the Greeks could hear her, "How long, ye simple ones, will ye back your oars?"

The order of the battle was this. The Phœnicians were on the right wing, towards the west and towards Eleusis, and the Athenians were ranged over against them; and the Ionians were on the left, toward the east and towards the Piræus, having the Lacedæmonians over against them. Of the Ionians a few only followed the counsel of Themistocles, and held back from the fighting; for many of their captains took ships of the Greeks, of whom was Theomestor, that for this service was made lord of Samos by the Persians, and Phylacus, who also was of Samos, that had lands given to him and was written among the benefactors of the King. But for the most part the ships of the Persians were destroyed by the Greeks, and especially by the Athenians and the men of Ægina. For the Greeks fought in good order and kept their plans, but the barbarians were without order, neither had they any purpose in what they did. Wherefore they must needs have been worsted in the battle. Nevertheless they this day surpassed themselves, bearing themselves more bravely than at Eubœa; for every man was very zealous, having the fear of the King before his eyes, and deeming that the King saw what he did.

How the rest of the Greeks and of the barbarians behaved themselves cannot be described, but of Artemisia of Halicarnassus this story is told. The fleet of the King being now in great confusion, it so chanced that the ship of Artemisia was pursued by an Athenian ship. And she, not being able to escape, for she was the nearest of all to the ships of the enemy, and had many of her own friends in front of her, devised this means of saving herself, and also accomplished it. She drave her ship against the ship of the lord of Calyndus, being one of the fleet of the King (whether she had a quarrel against this man, or the ship chanced to be in her way is not known for certain), and had the good fortune to sink it. And thus she gained a double gain. For when the captain of the Athenian ship saw what she did, judging that her ship was of the fleet of the Greeks, or that it had deserted from the King, he left pursuing her; and also, having done this ill service to the Persians, yet she got the greatest glory from the King. For Xerxes, as he looked upon the battle, saw not her ship smite another. And one said to him, "O King, seest thou how bravely Queen Artemisia bears herself, sinking a ship of the enemies?" Then said the King, "Was this verily the doing of Artemisia?" And they affirmed that it was, knowing the token of her ship; but the ship that was sunk they judged to be one of the Greeks. It so chanced also, that her good fortune might be complete, that not a man of the ship of Calyndus was left to tell the truth. As for Xerxes, he is reported to have said, "My men have become women, and my women have become men."

In this battle fell Ariabignes, being brother to the King, and also many other famous men of the Medes and the Persians. Of the Greeks indeed there perished not many; for even though their ships were destroyed, yet being able to swim they saved themselves; but of the barbarians the greater part perished, for they were not able to swim. And so soon as the first of the Persian ships began to fly before the Greeks then there followed a great destruction. For they that were behind pressed forward, seeking to show some deed of valor before the eyes of the King, and drave against the ships that fled, and so both did and received great damage. This thing also happened. Certain of the Phœnicians, whose ships had perished, came to the King and made a complaint against the Ionians that they had betrayed them. But while they were yet speaking, a ship of Samothrace drave against an Athenian ship and sank it; then there came a ship of Ægina against the ship of Samothrace and wounded it sorely; notwithstanding, while it was sinking the Samothracians, being throwers of javelins, smote down the men of Ægina, and boarded their ship and took possession of it. This thing was the salvation of the Ionians. For Xerxes, seeing that these Greeks had wrought a great deed and being in great vexation of spirit, and ready to blame all men, commanded that they should cut off the heads of the Phœnician captains, that they might not any more bring accusations against men that were better than they. All the time of the battle the King sat on the hill that is over against Salamis, and when any deed of valor was done by his ships, he would ask the name of the captain, and the scribes wrote it down, with the names also of his father and of his city.

Such of the ships of the barbarians as sought to escape by way of Phalerum the men of Ægina dealt with, waiting in the strait, and behaving themselves most valorously. For the Athenians destroyed such as yet fought and such as fled, and the men of Ægina fell upon them that would sail out, so that if any escaped the Athenians they fell into the hands of the men of Ægina.

In this battle the men of Ægina were judged to have shown most valor, and next to them the Athenians; and among the men of Ægina Polycritus, and among the Athenians Eumenes and Ameinias. It was this Ameinias that pursued Artemisia. And indeed, had he known whom he pursued, he would not have left following her till he had taken her, or himself been taken; for there was proclaimed a reward of ten thousand drachmas to the man that should take Artemisia alive, the Athenians being very wroth that a woman should presume to bear arms against their city.

Of Adeimantus the Corinthian the Athenians tell this story, that in the very beginning of the battle, being wholly mastered with fear, he hoisted his sails and fled; and that the other Corinthian ships, seeing the ship of their commander flying, fled also; and that when they were come in their flight over against the temple of Athene of Sciron, they met there a pinnace, that came not by any bidding of men; and that when it was close to their ships the men in the pinnace cried out, "Thou indeed art flying, O Adeimantus, and showing thyself traitor to the Greeks; but they are winning the victory over their enemies." When Adeimantus would not believe, the men said that they were willing to answer for it with their lives that their words were true. Then Adeimantus turned back his ship, and he and his companions came to Salamis when the battle was now finished. This is the story of the Athenians concerning the Corinthians; but the Corinthians deny it, affirming that they fought among the first. And in this they are confirmed by the testimony of the other Greeks.

On that day Aristides the Athenian did good service. He took with him many men at arms, Athenians, that had been drawn up along the shore of Salamis, and landed them on the island of Psyttaleia, so that they slew all the Persians that had been set to keep the place.

When the battle was ended the Greeks drew to Salamis such of the broken ships as yet floated, and prepared to fight yet again, for they thought that the King would not fail to use the ships that remained to him. But many of the wrecks the wind—for it chanced to blow from the west—carried to the shore of Attica, which is called the shore of Colias. Thus was fulfilled a certain oracle of Lysistratus the Athenian.

"That Colian dames their bread may bake,
Full many an oar that day shall break."

And this came to pass after the King had departed.

CHAPTER XIX

OF THE FLIGHT OF XERXES

WHEN King Xerxes perceived what damage his ships had suffered he resolved that he would flee without delay to Persia. Yet, to hide this purpose, he made as if he would carry on the war, making a mound across the channel that is between Salamis and the mainland, and doing other things. But though he deceived others he did not deceive Mardonius.

In the meanwhile he sent a messenger to Susa, whither he had before sent the tidings of how he was master of Athens, and as before the people had rejoiced, strewing myrtle boughs in the streets, and burning incense, and feasting and making merry, so now they were greatly troubled, rending their garments, and making much ado with weeping and wailing. Nor was it for the damage of the ship that they lamented, but for fear lest the King himself should suffer harm. Nor would they be comforted till he came back in safety.

Now when Mardonius saw that the King purposed to flee, fearing lest he should suffer punishment for that he had advised the marching against Greece, he made this resolve, that either he would himself conquer

Greece—and this indeed he hoped to do—or perish honorably. Wherefore he said to Xerxes, "Trouble not thyself overmuch, O master, for this loss that has befallen us; for these fellows, whom thou thinkest to have conquered us, will not dare to stand against us. And, if we wish, we may deal with them without delay, or, if we will, we may wait awhile. But if, O King, thou art minded to depart straightway, hear my counsel. Make not thy Persians a laughing-stock to the Greeks. For if the Phœnicians and Egyptians and the like have played the coward, yet have not the Persians so done. Depart then, therefore, if thou art so minded, but let me choose out three hundred thousand men of the army, with whom I may conquer these Greeks."

Xerxes when he heard these words was very glad, and made answer to Mardonius that he would deliberate about these things. And because before Artemisia only had perceived what should be done, he sent for her, and when she was come, sent away his other counselors, and inquired of her what he should do, setting before her the counsel of Mardonius. To this she made answer in these words: "I counsel thee to depart straightway, O King. And if Mardonius promises to conquer Greece for thee, let him stay behind and do it. For if he succeed, thine will be the gain; and if he fail, there will follow no great damage, so that thou and thy house be safe. For of a surety, so long as these remain, the Greeks will often be in peril of their lives. And if they prevail over this Mardonius, he is nothing more than thy slave." This counsel seemed very good to the King, being altogether to his mind; and if all the men and women in the world had counseled him to remain, hardly would he have done it, so terrified was he. He commended therefore Artemisia, and sent her on to Ephesus with certain of his children in her charge, in which charge was joined also one Hermotimus of Pedasus. The people of Pedasus say that when a mischance is about to befall any of their neighbors the priestess of Athene in their city has a beard, and that this has happened twice.

The next day Xerxes commanded the ships to sail with all speed to the Hellespont, that they might guard the bridges against his coming. So they departed; and sailing by Cape Zoster, where certain rocks jut out from the land, they took the rocks for ships, and fled far away. But afterward, when they knew the truth, they gathered themselves together again.

For awhile the Greeks, seeing the army of the barbarians in the same place, supposed that the ships also remained, and made ready for battle. But when they knew the truth, they pursued after them; but having sailed as far as Andros, and not seeing them, they held a council of war. Then Themistocles would have had them make with all speed for the Hellespont that they might break down the bridges, but Eurybiades was of the contrary opinion, saying, "There can no worse thing befall the Greeks than that we should break down the bridges. For if the Persians be thus cut off and driven to remain, see what will follow. If they be quiet they must come to ruin, for their host will perish of hunger; but if they bestir themselves they will conquer all Europe, city by city, and for food they will have our harvests. Now, indeed, because his ships have been vanquished, he is minded to depart; and this we should suffer him to do. Only when he has departed, we may, if we will, strive with him for the mastery of his own country."

To this counsel the other leaders of the Peloponnesians consented. And when Themistocles saw that he could not persuade them, he changed his purpose, and said to the Athenians, for these were vexed beyond all the rest that the Persians were suffered to escape, "Often have I seen with my own eyes or heard from others that men having been worsted and driven to despair have recovered their own and become conquerors in their turn. Now we have found great good fortune, saving ourselves and Greece from this mighty host of men. Let us therefore be content and not pursue them when they flee. For we have not done this of our own might. The Gods and the heroes have done it, having jealousy that one man should be lord both of Asia and Europe, and he, too, a destroyer of images and temples, and that scourged the sea and threw fetters into it. Let us, therefore, now that the barbarians have departed, return each man to his home and sow our land, and in the spring will we sail to the Hellespont!"

With these words he persuaded the Athenians; but he did it that he might bind the King to him by this service, desiring to have a refuge, if any evil should come upon him at Athens. Wherefore he sent certain men to Attica, faithful men that would not betray him even under torture, and among them the man Sicinnus. This Sicinnus went to the King and said, "Themistocles the Athenian, wishing to do thee a service, has sent me to tell thee that he has restrained the Greeks who would have broken the bridges of the Hellespont, and that thou mayest return at thy leisure."

After this the Greeks laid siege to Andros. For Themistocles had demanded money of this city for the Greeks, saying "You must needs pay the money, for we come bringing with us two great gods, even Persuasion and Necessity." But the Andrians made answer, "Well may Athens be great and happy, seeing that it has such gods; but we have two that are unprofitable, yet dwell with us and will not leave us, even Poverty and Helplessness." For this cause the Greeks besieged their city. As for Themistocles, he ceased not to get riches for himself, without the knowledge of the others, taking money from the islanders and others that the fleet should not sail against them.

Meanwhile Mardonius chose out of the host such as he would have for his army. All the Immortals he chose, save Hydarnes, who was not willing to leave the King, and such of the Persians as wore corslets, and the thousand horsemen, and the Medes and the Sacæ and Bactrians and the Indians, both horse and foot. These nations he took wholly, and out of the rest of the host he chose such as excelled in stature or had done some valiant deed. The number was three hundred thousand in all. This choosing was done in Thessaly; and before it was finished there came a herald from Sparta, seeking satisfaction from the King for the death of Leonidas and his companions, for the god at Delphi had bidden the Spartans seek for it. The herald stood before Xerxes and said, "King of the Medes, the Spartans and the sons of Hercules ask of thee satisfaction for blood-guiltiness, because thou didst slay their King Leonidas when he defended Greece." The King laughed; but after a while he pointed to Mardonius, who chanced to be present, and said, "This man will give such satisfaction as is due." And the herald said, "I accept the satisfaction," and so departed.

After this Xerxes, leaving Mardonius in Thessaly, made for the Hellespont with all haste. In forty and five days he came to it, having but a small part of his army. These had laid their hands on all the corn in the countries through which they passed; and where corn was wanting they had devoured the bark and the leaves of all manner of trees, leaving nothing at all, so that many died of sundry diseases, and some were left behind sick in the cities on the way. When they came to the Hellespont they found the bridges broken, and crossed over in ships as they best could. And many, when they had abundance of food and drink, using these without measure, so died.

There is told another tale of the flight of Xerxes. He left Hydarnes, it is said, to have charge of the army, and himself embarked on a Phœnician ship, and so sailed to Asia. But as he sailed there fell upon the ship a great wind from the north; and, being overladen, it was ready to sink, for there were many Persians with the King upon the deck. Then Xerxes cried aloud to the helmsman, saying, "Is there any help?" And the helmsman answered, "There is no help except we be rid of these many passengers." Then said Xerxes to the Persians, "Let now any that will, show that he cares for his King, for my life is in your hands." Then the

Persians made obeisance to him and leaped into the sea; so the ship being lightened came safe to Asia. And when Xerxes was come to the shore he dealt thus with the helmsman. For that he had saved the life of the King he gave him a crown of gold; but for that he had caused the death of many Persians, he commanded that he should be beheaded. But this story is scarcely to be believed. For why did not the King rather send down these Persians, being the first men in the realm, into the lower part of the ship, and cause the like number of rowers, being Phœnicians, to leap into the sea? But in truth Xerxes returned by way of the land, whereof we have a proof that he passed through Abdera, and making a covenant with the people of that city, gave them a cimeter of gold and a turban broidered with gold.

And now the Greeks were assembled at the Isthmus that they might adjudge the prize of valor to him that of all the Greeks had shown himself most worthy in the war. The captains then being met laid their votes on the altar of Poseidon, a vote for the first place and a vote for the second. Each man gave the first place to himself, but the greater part gave the second to Themistocles. But though the captains could not agree for jealousy, yet was Themistocles commonly reported among Greeks to have shown himself by far the wisest man of all in the war. And when he went to Sparta the Spartans received him with great honor. The prize of valor indeed, which was a crown of olive, they gave to Eurybiades; but the prize of wisdom and dexterity, also a crown of olive, they gave to Themistocles. Also they gave him the fairest chariot that was in all Sparta; and when he departed three hundred chosen men, that are called the Knights, went with him so far as the borders of Tegea. Nor has any man, save Themistocles only, been so sent out of their country by the Spartans.

When he came back to Athens a certain citizen of Aphidnæ, that came from Belbis, being his enemy, a man of no repute, reproached him, saying, "Thou hast these honors from the Spartans for Athens' sake, not for thine own." And when the man said this many times, Themistocles answered him, "Surely I had not been so honored had I been of Belbis, nor thou hadst thou been of Athens."

CHAPTER XX

OF THE PREPARING OF THE PERSIANS AND OF THE GREEKS FOR THE WAR

MARDONIUS and his host had their winter quarters in Thessaly. When he was now about to leave them, he sent one Mys, a man of Caria, to inquire of the oracles. This Mys inquired of the oracles and of Amphiaraus in Thebes. (No Theban may inquire of Amphiaraus, for he gave them their choice whether they would have him for their prophet or their helper; and they chose to have him for their helper.) But when Mardonius read the answer that had been given to Mys, he sent an envoy to Athens, even Alexander of Macedon, choosing him because his sister was married to a Persian, and because he was a friend to the Athenians.

Of the ancestors of Alexander there is told this story. Three brothers of the royal house of Argos came into the land of Macedonia and took service with the King, one tending the horses, and one the cows, and one the smaller cattle. In those days not the people only but the kings also were poor, so that the King's wife was wont to bake the bread. And when she baked it she saw that the loaf of Perdiccas, that was the youngest of the brothers, grew to be twice as large as the other loaves. And as this happened day after day she told it to her husband. Then the man perceiving that it was a miracle, and signified no small matter, bade the three depart out of the country. But when they would have had their wages, he said to them, for it chanced that the sun was shining down the chimney into the house, "Here are your fit wages. This I give you;" and he pointed to the sunshine, for the Gods had taken his wits from him. The two elder stood astonished and said nothing, but the youngest, having a knife in his hand, drew a line with it on the floor round the sunshine, and made as if he would draw it up into his bosom three times, and so departed and his brothers with him. Now when they were gone, one went and told to the King what the youngest had done; and the King, when he heard it, was angry, and sent horsemen after them to slay them. But a certain river swelled so high when the three brothers of Argos had safely crossed it, that the horsemen could not follow. (Their descendants yet do sacrifice to this river as to their saviour.) The brothers took up their abode in a place which they call the Gardens of Midas. (Here are roses so great as can not be found elsewhere, having each sixty leaves, and over the gardens a mountain so cold that none can climb to the top.) From this place they went forth till they had conquered the whole land of Macedonia. From this Perdiccas came Alexander the Macedonian in the seventh generation.

Alexander said, "Men of Athens, Mardonius bids me say that there has come to him this message from the King, 'I forgive the Athenians all their trespasses against me. And do thou this, Mardonius. Give them back their land and add to it any other that they will, and build again the temples that I burned with fire, if they will make agreement with me. And they shall live under their own laws.' Mardonius also says, 'This will I do unless ye on your part hinder me. And why do ye stand out against the King? Do ye not know his might? See this great host that I have. If so be that ye prevail over this, which indeed ye can not hope to do, there will come against ye a host many times greater. Why then will ye resist, losing your country and going always in danger of your lives?' These are the words of Mardonius; and I, Alexander, for that I am your friend, beseech you to give ear to him, and to make agreement with the King, who has chosen you out of all the Greeks to make friendship and alliance with you."

Now the Spartans knew that Alexander had been sent by Mardonius to Athens. Whereupon they also sent ambassadors; and it was ordered that they should have audience of the people on the selfsame day. When therefore Alexander had spoken, the Spartans stood forth, and urged them that they should not listen to the words of Mardonius, nor betray the Greeks. Also they promised that they would give sustenance to their women and children so long as the war should continue. To Alexander the Athenians made this answer: "We know how great is the power of the barbarians, yet will we resist it to the uttermost, holding fast to our freedom. Seek not then to persuade us, but say to Mardonius, 'So long as the sun shall go by the path which now he goeth, we make no agreement with Xerxes, but will stand against him, the Gods and heroes whose temples he has burned with fire helping us.' And thou, Alexander, come not again to Athens with such words as these, for thou art our friend and we would not willingly do thee hurt."

To the Spartans they said, "It is like enough that ye should be fearful about this thing. Nevertheless ye, knowing what manner of men we are, did us great wrong. Know then there is no store of gold in all the world, nor land so fair that would tempt us to make agreement with the Persians. For first we can have no peace with them that have burned with fire our temples and the images of our Gods. And next we can not betray our brethren the Greeks that have one tongue with us and worship the same Gods. Know therefore that so long as one Athenian shall remain alive we will make no agreement with Xerxes. As for your kindness to us, we thank you; but we will not be burdensome to you. Only lead out your army with all speed. For we doubt not that the barbarians will invade our land a second time. Therefore should we meet him in Bœotia, and there join battle with him."

When Mardonius heard the words of the Athenians he marched forthwith into Attica, nor would he harken to the Thebans when they counseled him to tarry in Bœotia and seek to divide the Greeks against themselves. For they said, "If the Greeks be at one no power on earth can subdue them; but if thou wilt send gifts to the chief men in each state, thou wilt easily prevail." But Mardonius greatly desired to be master of

Athens a second time. This he did, but the Athenians had departed, some to their ships, but the greater part to Salamis.

After this he sent another messenger with the same words that Alexander of Macedonia had brought, for he thought, "Now that they have lost their country a second time they will surely listen to him." When the man—he was a Greek from the Hellespont—was brought into the council, a certain councilor, Lycidas, said, "Let us bring this matter before an assembly of the people." But when the Athenians, both the councilors and they that stood without, heard these words, they were full of wrath, and rose up against Lycidas, and stoned him with stones that he died. And the women ran with one accord to his house and slew his wife and his children in the same fashion. But the messenger the Athenians sent away without hurt.

A TORCH DANCE

Meanwhile the Athenians had sent ambassadors to Sparta, complaining that the Spartans had not sent an army to defend Attica from the barbarians. Now the Spartans were keeping holiday, for it was the feast of Hyacinthus, and had no thought for any thing besides. Also the wall which they were building across the Isthmus was now well advanced, so that they were putting on it the battlements. The ambassadors therefore, being brought in before the Ephors, said, "The King was willing to make peace with us, and to give us back our country, and to add to it any other country that we would. But we would not betray Greece, though we knew that it should be more to our profit to make peace with the Persians than to continue fighting against them. We therefore have been true to you, but ye have been false to us, caring nothing for us now that ye have come near to finish your wall across the Isthmus. But come; now that Bœotia is lost we shall best fight in the plain of Thria."

To these words the Ephors made no answer, but put off the matter to the morrow; and on the morrow they did likewise, and so for ten days.

But on the tenth day there came to the Ephors a man of Tegea, one Chileus, that had more weight with the Spartans than any other stranger. This Chileus said, "The matter stands thus, ye Ephors. If the Athenians be not your friends but make agreement with the Persians, then how strong soever shall be your wall across the Isthmus, there will be many doors open into the Peloponnese. Hearken therefore to what these men say while it is time."

This counsel they took to heart. To the ambassadors they said nothing, but that same night they sent five thousand Spartans, and with each seven helots, their captain being Pausanias, the son of Cleombrotus. The next day the ambassadors came unto the Ephors, being minded to depart to their own country, and said, "Ye Spartans stay at home and keep holiday and leave the Greeks to perish. We Athenians will make agreement with the King, and will go with him whithersoever he will lead us."

To this the Ephors made answer with an oath, "The men are gone against the strangers (for they called the barbarians *strangers*), and are now in Oresteum of Arcadia." When the ambassadors heard this they also departed; and at the same time there went five thousand men of Laconia, chosen men and fully armed.

When the men of Argos knew that the Spartans had departed they sent a messenger to Mardonius, the swiftest runner they could find—for they had promised to keep the Spartans from coming—saying, "The Spartans have set forth, neither could we stay them. Take heed therefore to thyself." When Mardonius heard this he would tarry no longer in Attica, but departed straightway, having first burned with fire and destroyed all that yet stood, whether house or temple. For Attica was not fit for horsemen, and if he should be worsted in the battle, there was no escape save by one narrow pass only. Wherefore he was minded to go back into Bœotia, for this country was fit for horsemen, and also was the country of friends. But while he was on his way there came another messenger saying that there were a

thousand Spartans in the land of Megara, having come
in advance of the army; and, thinking that he might
cut them off, he changed his purpose and marched
toward Megara, while the horsemen ravaged the
country. Nor did the Persians make their way toward
the setting sun further than this. And now there came
another messenger saying that the whole army of the
Peloponnesians was at the Isthmus. Therefore he turned
his course, and came into the territory of the Thebans.
And here he encamped his army along the river Asopus
from Erythræ to Platæa. And though the Thebans were
friends to the Persians, he cut down all the trees in the
country, not from hatred but from need, because he
would have a rampart and a place of refuge if the battle
should go against him. Such a rampart he made of ten
furlongs every way.

While the Persians were building this defense a
certain Theban made a great feast to Mardonius and the
Persians. Concerning this feast Thersander, a notable
citizen of Orchomenus, told this story to Herodotus: "I
was called to this feast with other Thebans, fifty in all,
and there were called also fifty Persians. We were not
set apart, but on each couch a Persian and a Theban;
and when we had dined and were now drinking, the
Persian that was on the same couch said to me in the
Greek tongue. 'Whence art thou?' and I said, 'I am
of Orchomenus.' Then said he, 'Since thou hast eaten
with me from the same table and poured out a libation
from the same cup, I will leave with thee a memorial
of my belief, and this the more that thou mayest look
after thine own life. Thou seest these Persians that are

feasting with us and this army that we left encamped on the river. Of all these thou shalt see in a short time but few remaining.' And when the Persian had so spoken he wept bitterly. And I said to him, for I marveled much at his words, 'Shouldst thou not tell this to Mardonius and to the Persians that are in high place with him?' But the Persian answered, 'O my friend, that which the Gods order a man can not change, for though he speak the truth no one will hearken to him. Many of the Persians know these things that I have said unto thee, but are constrained by necessity to follow whither we are led. But of all the griefs in man's life none is so sore as this, to know much and to have power to do nothing.' "

This story did Thersander tell to Herodotus, as he told it to many others also, even before the battle of Platæa.

CHAPTER XXI

OF THE BATTLE OF PLATÆA

THE Spartans pitched their camp at the Isthmus, whither came the other men of the Peloponnese also, so many as followed the good cause, not being willing to be left behind when the Spartans went forth to the war. And from the Isthmus they marched to Eleusis. Here the Athenians, having crossed over from Salamis came up with him. When they saw that the barbarians were encamped on the Asopus, they ranged themselves over against them on the slope of Mount Cithæron. Here Mardonius sent his cavalry under Masistius their captain to attack them. This Masistius was in great repute among the Persians, and he rode on a horse of Nisa, that had a bit of gold, and was otherwise richly adorned. The horsemen charged the Greeks by squadrons, and did them much damage.

Now it so chanced that the men of Megara had been set in the place where the cavalry could most easily approach; and these, as they received much damage, sent a message to Pausanias, saying, "Send over and help us, for without help we can not hold our place." Then Pausanias inquired whether any would take the place of the men of Megara, but none were willing, save the Athenians only. Of these, three hundred chosen men, having with them the archers, took the place of the men of Megara. And after a while, the barbarians still charging by squadrons it chanced that an arrow struck the horse of Masistius on the flank, he being a long way in front of the others. And the horse reared by reason of the pain and threw off its rider; which when the Athenians saw, they ran forward and slew Masistius where he lay. For a while they could not kill him, for he had a breast-plate of scales of gold and a tunic of scarlet over it, and this could not be broken through by any blows; which when one of the soldiers perceived he drave his weapon into the man's eye and so slew him. When the Persians saw that he was dead they charged with their whole force, seeking to get back his dead body, and the Athenians, on the other hand, called to their comrades to help them. So the battle waxed hot; and while the three hundred were alone they could not hold their ground; but the others coming up, the Persians turned their backs, and, being now without a leader, returned to the camp.

Mardonius and the Persians made a great lamentation over Masistius, cutting the hair from their heads, and the manes from their horses and beasts of burden, and making all Bœotia resound with their crying, for they had lost a man whom the army honored next after Mardonius himself. But the Greeks put the dead body in a cart, and caused it to be carried through the army, and indeed it was worthy to be looked at, both for beauty and for stature. The cause why it was thus carried was that the men would leave their ranks to look at it.

THE STORY OF THE PERSIAN WAR

After this it seemed good to the Greeks to leave their place on the slopes of Cithæron and to come down to the territory of the Platæans. Here they set themselves in array, nation by nation, nigh to the fountain of Gargaphia and the precincts of the hero Andocrates, and they stood partly on certain small hillocks and partly on the plain.

But while the army was being set in array there arose a very sharp contention between the Athenians and the men of Tegea, who should be set on the left wing. The men of Tegea affirmed that this place had always been theirs of right, saying, "When first the sons of Hercules came back to the Peloponnese we, with others that then dwelt therein, went forth to meet them. Then Hyllus the son of Hercules said, 'There is no need to put these two armies in peril. Let the men of the Peloponnese choose a champion that he may fight with me.' And an agreement was made, 'If Hyllus slay the champion of the Peloponnesians, the children of Hercules shall return to their inheritance; but if the champion of the Peloponnesians slay Hyllus, then will the children of Hercules swear an oath that they will not again seek to return for the space of a hundred years.' Then Echemus, that was King of Tegea, offered himself for champion, and slew Hyllus in battle. For this cause we have always had our place in one of the wings when the men of the Peloponnese go forth to battle."

To this the Athenians made answer, "We are come hither not to make speeches but to fight against the barbarians. But as the men of Tegea will have a comparison of deeds we must of necessity set forth

190

our claims. To the children of Hercules, whose leader they affirm themselves to have slain, we alone of all the Greeks gave shelter; and when the Thebans would not give up for burial the bodies of the Argives that had been slain in the siege of their city, we took them and buried them at Eleusis, and we fought against the Amazons, and in the war of Troy were not one whit behind any. But why should we speak of ancient things? Surely for what we did at Marathon, when we, alone of all the Greeks, fought against the Persians, and conquered them, putting to flight forty and six nations, we are worthy to have this honor, yea, and many other honors also. Nevertheless—for at such a time it is not fitting to dispute about places—we are ready to do as ye command, ye men of Sparta, and take our place wheresoever ye will, and there quit ourselves like men."

Then all the Spartans cried out with one voice that the Athenians were the more worthy to have the place.

The whole number of the Greeks was of heavy-armed men thirty-eight thousand and seven thousand, and of light-armed sixty and nine thousand.

Mardonius also set his battle in array. Over against the Spartans he set the Persians; and since these far excelled the Spartans in number he drew them up with their ranks deeper than common, and also so ordered it that they stood opposite to the men of Tegea; only the best of them he set to deal with the Spartans. Next to the Persians he set the Medes, and next to the Medes the

Bactrians. These stood over against the other dwellers in the Peloponnese. But against the Athenians he set such of the Greeks and Macedonians as had joined themselves to him.

Both armies being now ready for battle, the soothsayers offered sacrifice. The Spartans had with them one Tisamenus, a man of Elis. To this Tisamenus, inquiring about his childlessness, there was given an oracle that he should be the winner in five very great contests. This he understood of the contests of the games. But when he had exercised himself for the fivefold contests at Olympia but had failed, being vanquished in wrestling by a man of Andros, the Spartans perceived that the oracle spake not of contests in sport but of contests in battle. Then they sought to hire the man that he might go with them to battle. But he said, "Give me the citizenship of your city." This they could not endure, but when the fear of the Persians hung over them they sent to him again. And Tisamenus, perceiving that they were changed, said, "Ye must give the citizenship not to me only but to my brother also." To them only have the Spartans given their citizenship. So Tisamenus offered sacrifice, and the signs were for good luck if the Greeks staid in their place, but for bad if they crossed the Asopus.

To Mardonius also were given the same signs when he sacrificed before the battle. For he too had a soothsayer, who divined after the Greek manner, a certain Hegistratus of Elis. This man had been taken by the Spartans and condemned to die, but set himself free in a marvelous way. The Spartans had set him with

THE SACRIFICE

one foot in the stocks, these being of wood, but bound with iron. But some one giving him a tool of iron, he cut off with his own hand so much of his foot that he could draw that which was left through the hole. And after making his way through the woods, for he was watched by watchmen, he escaped to Tegea, traveling by night and hiding himself in the woods by day. And though the whole people of the Spartans sought for him he came safe on the third night to Tegea; for Tegea was in those days at enmity with Sparta. And now he served Mardonius right willingly, partly for gain, and partly for hatred of the Spartans.

And for eight days the two armies sat over against each other doing nothing, save that the horsemen of the Persians laid hands on a convoy of five hundred beasts that brought food from the Peloponnese to the Greeks.

Again they sat quiet for two days. On the eleventh day the Persians held a council. Then Artabazus, a man held in high esteem among the Persians, said, "Let us break up our camp, and bring our army to Thebes, where is a fenced city, and food in plenty for ourselves and our beasts. And when we are there, seeing we have gold, coined and uncoined, in abundance, and silver, and cups, let us take of these without stinting and send gifts to the Greeks, especially to them that bear rule in the cities. Speedily will they give up their freedom."

But Mardonius, being of a contrary opinion, was very fierce and obstinate, saying, "We are much stronger than they. Therefore let us fight as speedily as may be. As for the signs of the soothsayer we will not heed them, but will give battle as the Persians are wont to do." And the opinion of Mardonius prevailed, for it was he that was captain of the host.

That night came Alexander of Macedon to the camp of the Greeks and desired to speak with the generals. Then ran some of the guards and said, "Here is come a horseman from the camp of the Persians, who would speak with the generals, naming them by name." And when these had gone to the outposts they found Alexander, who said to them, "Men of Athens, tell to no man, save to Pausanias only, what I shall say unto you. For surely I had not come but that I had a great love for Greece; and indeed I am a Greek by descent, but would fain see this land free rather than enslaved. Hear, therefore. Mardonius can not get the signs as he would have them; else he would have given battle long since. But now he is minded not to heed the signs any more but to fight. Be ye not then taken unawares, but make ready to receive him. But if he still delay, then abide in your place, for he can not long hold out, having but a few days' provision. And if the end of this war be as ye would have it, remember me and the kindness I have done you. I am Alexander the Macedonian." When he had so spoken he rode back to his own people.

After this Pausanias said to the Athenians, "It would be well that you should deal with the Persians, of whom ye have had experience, having prevailed over them at Marathon, and we with the Boeotians and the other Greeks. For we know nothing of the Persians and of their manner of fighting, but the Greeks we know well. Let us therefore go to our place in the line, and ye shall come to yours."

The Athenians answered, "We had this very thing in our minds, and would have spoken ourselves, but that we doubted whether it would please you. But now let it be done."

So Pausanius, it being now morning, began to lead his men to the left wing. But the Thebans perceiving it, told it to Mardonius, who changed his order also, which, when Pausanius saw, he led the Spartans back and stood as before. Then Mardonius sent a herald to the Spartans, saying, "Ye said that ye are braver than other men, never leaving your place, but remaining till ye slay your enemies or are yourselves slain. But this we now see to be false; for ye leave your place before ever the battle is joined. But come now. Will ye fight with an equal number of Persians, ye for the Greeks and they for the King?" When the herald had waited a while, and no man answered him a word, he departed.

Then Mardonius, being greatly puffed up by this

PLATAEA

victory of words, commanded his horsemen that they should charge the Greeks. This they did, doing much damage with the throwing of javelins and the shooting of arrows, for they used the bow while they rode, so that the Greeks could not deal with them hand to hand. Also they choked the fountain of Gargaphia, from which all the Greeks drew water. The Spartans only had their place near to the fountain, but all the Greeks used it, for the horsemen and the archers of the barbarians kept them from the river. Then the captains held a council; and it seemed good to them, if the Persians should not fight that day, to change the place of their camp to the Island. This is before the city of Platæa, and men call it the Island because a certain river, coming down from Mount Cithæron, divides here into two streams which flow for a space three furlongs apart, and after join together again. So all that day they stood in their place, suffering grievously from the horsemen of the barbarians, and when it was night they began to change their place. And when the greater part of the Greeks had departed—but they went not to the Island, but fled straight to Platæa, and encamped by the temple of Here, which is before the city—Pausanias commanded the Spartans that they also should depart. The rest of the captains were willing to obey, but one Amompharetus, that led the men of Pitana, would not move, saying, "I will not fly from the strangers, nor bring disgrace upon Sparta." Pausanius took it very ill that the man should not obey his command, yet he would not leave him and his company alone, lest they should be destroyed. For this cause he kept the Spartans and their army in its place, and sought to persuade Amompharetus. And when the Athenians saw that the rest of the Greeks had departed, but that the Spartans remained, knowing that it was their custom to think one thing and say another, they sent a horseman to inquire whether they were minded to go or to remain. When the horseman came he found them in the very heat of the dispute, for Amompharetus took up a very great stone with both his hands and laid it at the feet of Pausanias, saying, "With this pebble I vote not to fly from the strangers" (for the Greeks give their votes with pebbles), and Pausanias affirmed that he was a fool and mad. And turning himself to the Athenian horseman, he said, "Ye see how things are with us; go and tell this to your captains." So the men departed; but the Spartans ceased not to dispute till the day began to dawn. And then Pausanias gave the signal to depart, expecting that

Amompharetus, when he found that they had departed, would also leave his place and follow them. And in this he judged rightly, for the man, thinking that he had been in truth forsaken, commanded his men that they should take their arms and follow the rest of the army. This they did, and came up with them in the space of ten furlongs, near to the temple of Demeter of Eleusis; for the army had waited for them there. The Athenians also left their place, but these marched all along the plain, while the Spartans kept to the hill for fear of the horsemen of the Persians.

When Mardonius heard that the Greeks had departed in the night, and beheld their place that it was empty, he called the sons of Aleuas, and said to them, "What say ye now, seeing this place is empty? Ye would have it that the Spartans fled from no man; yet ye saw before how they would have left their station, and now in this night now passed they have fled altogether. You indeed I can excuse, for ye know nothing of the Persians; but I marvel at Artabanus that he feared these men, and would have had us follow a coward's counsel, even to break up our camp, and to suffer ourselves to be besieged in the city of Thebes. Verily the King shall hear of this matter. And indeed we must not suffer them to do as they would, but must pursue after them till we overtake them, and exact punishment for all the wrong that they have done."

When he had thus spoken he led the Persians across the Asopus, and followed the Spartans at full speed, as if they were verily flying from him; the Athenians he saw not, for they were hidden from him by the hills.

And the other barbarians, when they saw the Persians moving, took up their standards and came after them, as quickly as they could, without any order, as though they would have swallowed up the Greeks.

When Pausanais saw that the horsemen of the Persians were pressing him hard, he sent a messenger to the Athenians, saying, "Now that the hour is come when we must fight for Greece, whether she shall be enslaved or free, we and you, men of Athens, are all alone, for our allies have fled. We must therefore help the one the other as best we may. If these horsemen had fallen on you, then had we and the men of Tegea—for they are faithful to Greece—have helped you; and now must ye help us; and because we know that ye have been more zealous than any other nation in this present war, we ask you with the more confidence."

When the Athenians heard these words they made ready to go to the help of the Spartans; but the Greeks that fought for the King fell on them and hindered them. The Spartans therefore being left alone, made ready to fight against Mardonius and the Persians. But for a while the signs did not favor them, and while they tarried many fell, and many more were wounded, for the Persians had made a rampart of wicker shields and shot their arrows from behind it, troubling the Spartans grievously. But still the signs were evil, till Pausanias, lifting up his eyes to the temple of Here of Platæa, cried aloud, "O goddess, disappoint not the hopes of the Greeks." And as he prayed, the men of Tegea ran forward, and the Spartans—for at last the signs favored them—advanced also. The Persians left shooting and came to meet them. First there was fighting at the rampart of the wicker shields; and when this was broken down a very fierce battle by the temple of Demeter, wherein they fought against each other hand to hand. Many a time did the barbarians lay hold of the spears of the Greeks, seeking to break them; for in courage and strength the Persians were not one whit behind the Greeks, only they had not armor of defense, and were unused to battle, nor any match for their enemies in skill; but running forward, now one by one, and now in companies of ten, or, it might be, of more or less, threw themselves upon the Spartans, and so perished. Where Mardonius himself fought, riding on a white horse, having about him the thousand who were the bravest of all the Persians, the Greeks were hardest pressed. So long indeed as Mardonius lived his men held out, and smote down not a few of the Spartans; but when he had fallen and his companions with him, the rest of the Persians fled before the Greeks, for their equipment, being without armor, was a grievous hindrance to them. And indeed they were light-armed men, fighting with heavy-armed.

Thus did Mardonius and his host pay due penalty for the death of Leonidas, and Pausanias won a victory more glorious than any man had ever won before. As for Mardonius himself, he was slain by one Aeimnestus, that perished afterward, he and three hundred Spartans with him, fighting against the whole host of the Messenians.

The Persians, being now put to flight by the Spartans, fled without any order to their camp, to the defense of trees which they had made. As to the precinct of Demeter, though many fell round about it, none fell within it, or so much as entered it, the goddess, it is to be supposed—if it is lawful to suppose any thing about the Gods—herself keeping them from it, because they had burned her dwelling at Eleusis.

Artabazus having sought to hinder Mardonius from giving battle, when he found that he could not prevail, took counsel for his own safety. He commanded his men, of whom he had forty thousand, to follow at such speed as they should perceive him to use. Then he made as if he would have joined the battle, but seeing the Persians already in fight, he turned round and made with all speed for the Hellespont.

As for the Greeks that fought for the King, they all played the coward of set purpose, saving the Bœotians. These fought very fiercely with the Athenians, so that three hundred of them were slain.

Of the rest of the barbarians some stood against the Greeks, but fled so soon as they saw the Persians giving way. Nevertheless the horsemen, both Persian and Theban, did good service, coming between them that fled and the Greeks.

As for the rest of the Greeks, none did good service save the Spartans, and the Athenians, and the men of Tegea only. For when they heard that Pausanias prevailed, they hastened from Platæa with great haste and without order, which a captain of the Theban horsemen perceiving, he charged the men of Megara and of Phlius, that were marching along the plain, and slew six hundred of them, and drave the rest to Mount Cithæron. So these men perished without honor.

The men of Mantinea and of Elis came when the battle was now finished, greatly lamenting that they were late. These, when they had returned to their cities, banished their captains.

For none of the Greeks fought in this battle of Platæa save the Spartans and the Athenians and the men of Tegea only.

Now the Persians that had fled to the camp were able to climb into the towers before the Spartans came up; and being there, they held the wall as best they could. And indeed before the coming of the Athenians the barbarians kept back the Spartans, who are but little skilled in fighting against fortified places. But after the coming of the Athenians the wall was attacked yet more fiercely than before. These after a while prevailed, climbing to the top of the wall, and making a breach, so that the Greeks could enter in. And of all the Greeks the first to enter were the men of Tegea. These spoiled the tent of Mardonius, taking therefrom the mangers of brass from which his horses had eaten. And so the barbarians held out no longer, but were slaughtered as sheep, so that of the whole host there were left three thousand only. But Artabazus had taken with him forty thousand. Of the Spartans there perished ninety and one; of the men of Tegea sixteen; of the Athenians fifty and two.

Of the barbarians the bravest were the Persians among the foot soldiers, and the Sacæ among the horsemen; but of all Mardonius fought the best. Among the Greeks the Spartans excelled, and among the Spartans Aristodemus, that had come back from Thermopylæ, and Posidonius and Philocyon and Amompharetus. But of Aristodemus the Spartans said that he had manifestly sought for death by reason of his disgrace, and they paid no honor to him; but to the others that had not desired to die they paid honor.

As for Callicrates, that was the goodliest man not among the Spartans only, but among all the Greeks, he was slain, but not in the battle. For while Pausanias was sacrificing, and he sat in his place in the ranks, an arrow smote him in the side. Therefore, when his comrades went forward to the battle, men carried him out of the battle, being very loth to die, for he said to a Platæan that stood by, "It does not trouble me that I die for Greece, but that I die without putting my hand to the fight, or doing such worthy deeds as I had desired." Of the Athenians the bravest was Sophanes of Decelea, of whom they say that he had an anchor fastened to his belt by a chain of brass; and that when he came near to the enemy, he threw out his anchor so that he might not be able to be driven from his post; and that when the enemy fled, he took up his anchor and pursued. But others say he had the device of an anchor on his shield.

Of Pausanias they tell this story, that coming into the camp of the Persians, he found the war-tent of Xerxes, for Xerxes had left it with Mardonius. And when he saw it with its furniture of gold and silver, and adorned with hangings of divers colors, he commanded the bakers and the cooks that they should prepare a feast as they were wont to do for Mardonius. And when he saw the couches of gold and silver with their dainty coverlets, and tables of gold and silver, and all the furniture of the feast very rich, he was astonished; and for mirth's sake bade his servants prepare a dinner in the Spartan fashion. When they had so done, Pausanias laughed, seeing how great was the difference between them; and, sending for the other captains of the Greeks, he said to them, "I have brought you here that I may show you the folly of these Persians, who, having such fare as this, came to rob us of our poverty."

CHAPTER XXII

OF THE BATTLE AT MYCALE

WHILE these things were being done in the land of Bœotia, the fleet of the Greeks lay at Delos, Leotychides of Sparta being its chief captain; but the fleet of the Persians was at Samos. And there came from Samos three men whom the people of the land sent to the captains of the Greeks; but neither did the Persians know of their going, nor Theomestor the lord of the land, for the Persians had made him lord.

When these men were come into the presence of the captains, they were very urgent with them, saying, "If the Ionians do but see you, they will revolt from the Persians; nor will these abide your coming; or, if they abide it, ye will find such a prey as ye could not find elsewhere. It is right that ye should help men that are Greeks and worship the same gods. Right is it and easy withal, for the ships of the Persians are no match for yours. And if ye doubt whether we come in good faith, take us with you in your ships as hostages."

Then Leotychides asked the chief speaker of the three, "Man of Samos, what is thy name?" asking either because he sought for a sign or by chance and by inspiration of God. And the man said, "Hegesistratus," which is by interpretation "Leader of armies." Then said Leotychides, "I accept the sign of this word—leader of armies. Only you must pledge your word, you and these others, that the men of Samos will be zealous and true." Then the three pledged their word with an oath. And the Greeks sailed to Samos, taking with them Hegesistratus, for they took his name for a good sign. Also they had with them a soothsayer, one Deiphonus, the son of Evenius of Apollonia. Of Evenius they tell this story. The men of Apollonia have a flock of sheep that are sacred to the sun. And these feed by day by the river that flows from Mount Lacmon, and by night they are kept by men wealthy and noble, chosen from among the citizens, each man keeping them a year; for the men of Apollonia by reason of a certain oracle make much account of these sheep. They are folded by night in a cave that is far distant from the city; and it chanced that this Evenius, having the charge of them on a certain night, fell asleep, and that while he slept wolves entered into the caves and devoured sixty of them. Evenius indeed sought to keep the matter secret, purposing to put another sixty in the place of these, but it came to the knowledge of the people; and they brought him to judgment for his misdeed and condemned him to lose his eyes. But lo! after they had blinded him, the sheep bare no more any young, nor the land its wonted increase. And when the men of Apollonia inquired the cause of the oracle of Dodona, the prophet answered them, "Ye have done wickedly, blinding Evenius, the keeper of the sheep. The Gods sent these wolves; nor will they cease to avenge the man's cause till ye shall make him such satisfaction as he shall himself demand of you. And when ye have done this, then will the Gods themselves give him such a gift that all men shall call him blessed."

When this oracle came to them, the men of Apollonia kept the matter close, and sent certain citizens to make an agreement with Evenius. This agreement they made in this wise. They found Evenius sitting on a bench. Then they sat down by him, and when they had spoken of other things, came at the last to condole with him for his mishap. And they asked him, saying, "Evenius, if the men of Apollonia were minded to give thee satisfaction for this injury, what wouldst thou demand?" Now Evenius had not heard of the oracle, and he said, "If they will give me such and such lands," and he named the two citizens that he knew to have the best lands in the country, "and such a house," and he named a house that he knew to be the fairest in the whole city, "I will lay aside my wrath, holding that I have had due satisfaction." Then they that sat by him answered, "Evenius, the men of Apollonia give thee the satisfaction that thou demandest, according to the words of the oracle." Evenius, indeed, was very wroth when he heard the whole matter, and knew how he had been deceived; but the men of Apollonia bought the lands and the house from them that possessed them and gave to Evenius the things which he had desired. Immediately after this there fell upon him a gift of prophecy, so that he became famous throughout Greece. Deiphonus, son of this Evenius, was now soothsayer to the Greeks. But some say that Deiphonus was not truly his son, but had taken his name and plied the trade of a soothsayer for hire.

The Greeks, finding the signs to be good, sailed to Samos; but when the Persians knew of their coming they left their place and sailed to the mainland, having first sent away the ships of the Phœnicians, for they judged that they could not meet the Greeks in battle, and they desired to have the help of their army that was on the mainland; for Xerxes had left at Mycale, that is over against Samos, sixty thousand men, under Tigranes, a Persian of notable beauty and stature, to keep guard over Ionia.

So the captains of the Persian ships came to Mycale, and drew their ships up on the shore and made a fence round them of stones and wood, cutting down the fruit trees that were in the place, and setting stakes in the ground about the fence.

When the Greeks knew that the barbarians had fled to the mainland, they were greatly troubled that the men had escaped out of their hands, and doubted whether they should go home or sail to the Hellespont. But in the end they did neither the one thing nor the other, but sailed to the mainland, having got ready boarding bridges and other things needful for a sea-fight. But when they were come to the place, there were none to meet them, but they saw the ships drawn up within the ramparts, and a great army sat in array along the shore. First of all Leotychides sailed in his ship along the shore, keeping as close to the shore as might be, and crying with a loud voice, "Men of Ionia that chance to hear me, listen to that which I now say, for the Persians will understand none of my words. When we join battle, remember all of you first Freedom, and then our watchword, and this is Hebe. And if there are any that chance not to hear me, let others tell my words to them." Now the purpose of these words was the same as of the words which Themistocles wrote upon the rocks at Artemisium. If they came not to the knowledge of the Persians, then they might persuade the Ionians; but if they came to their knowledge they would cause the Persians to put no trust in their allies. When Leotychides had ended speaking these words, the allies brought their ships to the land and disembarked, and set themselves in array for the battle.

But the Persians, when they saw how the Greeks set themselves in array, considered the words which had been spoken to the Ionians. And first of all they took away from the men of Samos their arms, suspecting that they favored the Greeks. This they did because the men of Samos had paid the ransom of five hundred Athenians whom the armies of the King had found lingering in the land of Attica, and had carried away captive into Asia. Next after this they sent the men of Miletus to keep the ways that led to the heights of Mycale, for they knew the country. This they said, but in truth they desired to keep them outside the camp. Thus did the Persians seek to guard themselves against the Ionians, if these were minded to help the Greeks; and after this they made a rampart of wicker shields to be a defense against the enemy.

And now the Greeks, all things being ready, began to go forward against the barbarians. And lo! as they went there ran a rumor through the whole army and at the same time they saw a herald's staff lying on the sea-shore. And the rumor was this, that the Greeks were doing battle in the land of Bœotia with the army of Mardonius, and were prevailing over it. And this is one of the many proofs that the gods have a thought for the affairs of men; for how else, when it had chanced that this battle at Mycale and the ruin that fell on the Persians at Platæa should fall out on the selfsame day, came this rumor to the Greeks making them to be of a good courage and willing to put their lives in jeopardy? At Platæa the battle was in the morning, and at Mycale it was toward evening. And before the rumor came they had been fearful, not so much for themselves as for the Greeks, lest they should flee before Mardonius. But now their fear ceased, and they ran forward both quicker and with better courage. And indeed both the barbarians and the Greeks had much eagerness for the battle, whereof the prize was the Hellespont and the islands.

Now the Athenians and they that were with them, being altogether one-half the army, marched along the shore where the way was level, but the Lacedæmonians with the rest of the army marched over hills and the channel of a stream. And thus it came to pass that while these were making their compass the Athenians had now joined battle. So long as the wicker rampart was standing the Persians held their own and were not worsted in the fight; but when the Athenians and their fellows, desiring to have the victory for themselves, encouraged each other and attacked the Persians more fiercely, things went otherwise. For the Greeks burst through the rampart and fell in one body upon the Persians. These indeed awaited their coming and held out for a time, but at last fled into the fort. And the Athenians with the men of Corinth and of Sicyon and of Trœzen—for these had been set next to the Athenians—entered into the fort along with them. And now when their fort was taken, the barbarians made no more resistance, but fled all of them, save the Persians only. But while these still held out against the Greeks, a few fighting together, there came up the Lacedæmonians and the others, and slew them all. Not a few of the Greeks fell in this battle, especially among the men of Sicyon.

The men of Samos, from whom the Persians had taken their arms, did good service to the Greeks while they were fighting. As for the men of Miletus, they did not what had been commanded them, but led the Persians astray, so that they went into the hands of the enemy, and at last fell upon them with their own hands. Thus did Ionia revolt that day a second time from the King.